HERMES
AND
THE AKASHIC RECORDS
A GUIDE TO NAVIGATING THE AKASHIC RECORDS WITH HERMES

DAVID THOMPSON

HERMES
AND
THE AKASHIC RECORDS
A GUIDE TO NAVIGATING THE AKASHIC RECORDS WITH HERMES

DAVID THOMPSON

TRANS MUNDANE
PUBLISHING
—— OCCULT KNOWLEDGE ——

To Yellow-hair Buck, A shaman I knew back in Texas.

A Warning:

This is very powerful material. When worked properly, you may see unexpected results. These rituals and petitions are like electricity, the energy will flow in the direction of the intended output. In saying this, please be firm in your intentions and make absolutely sure what you want is truly want you desire.

As they say, be careful what you wish for, you just might get it.

"People assume that time is a strict progression of cause to effect, but actually, from a nonlinear, non-subjective viewpoint, it's more like a big ball of wibbly-wobbly, timey-wimey... stuff."

- The Tenth Doctor

CHAPTER ONE

About Me

Hello, I'm Dave Thompson.

You may be new to my books. I'm an Amazon best-selling author in the field of the occult and mystical studies. You may know me for my popular series, "High Magik Studies," which serves as a crucial guide for anyone interested in ceremonial magick. I also have a series on Roman/Greco magik, and a series on Norse magik is planned. My writing extends beyond occult literature to adult fantasy, most notably through my series, "The Furies."

My journey into High Magick began in the 1970s, and I've spent decades rigorously studying and practicing this art. I took a brief break to channel my magickal skills into a successful photography career. That venture led me to the bustling art scene of Los Angeles, where I worked as a photographer for various high-profile magazines.

In 2018, I made the decision to democratize High Magick by releasing a three-part instructional course. My unique teaching approach has made this esoteric art accessible to thousands of students worldwide, cultivating a new generation of magicians who understand its complexities.

But my talents are not confined to this realm alone. I've been a recognized medium and psychic since the rise of the psychic hotline era. I've offered psychic consultations and readings through various platforms, providing spiritual insights to many seeking answers.

I also dabble in screenwriting and production management. My screenplay, "Trouble Enough," was recognized as one of the "Top Ten Comedies" by the Screen Arts Foundation for Screenwriters in 2002. Whether I'm in LA or Austin, my extensive industry knowledge makes me a jack-of-all-trades in the entertainment world.

My spiritual journey began at the age of 13 when I had my first supernatural encounter. It was with a high-level spirit guide in my grandmother's home, an experience that both terrified and fascinated me. This led me to explore various spiritual disciplines, including the Akashic records and past and parallel lives. Completing a course in hypnosis induction under Richard Sutphen has only enriched my spiritual toolkit.

My life story is not just about my own transformative

journey, but also serves as a guiding light for others on their own spiritual quests.

My own journey to the Akashic records began in the early 2000s. It was shortly after learning to meditate and contact my guides. In a vivid dream, I was taken to a huge building, with a classic dome as the roof, marble fluted columns at the top of a huge set of steps leading to the main doors. A young man escorted me and introduced himself as Thoth/Hermes.

Taking my hand, he escorted me inside the building with a friendly smile. The sight before me was awe-inspiring as I gazed upon thousands of rows of bookshelves. The scenery was breathtaking, with the land stretching out endlessly before me, as far as I could see. He took me to a separate room, and inside this room was a long table. On this table, he told me was my current recording of my life thus far.

It wasn't a scroll or heavy book. It was a clear block, like crystal, at least twenty feet long (7 meters). Inside looked like the traces of a bullet, leaving several silvery paths. Along the main path were several side paths, but they eventually wound around and back to the center.

He explained the large path line was the path of my current lifetime. The smaller threads were my PLANNED paths, and notice how I deviated and wandered around, instead of sticking to my chosen path.

He explained how we all have free will, and can freely choose to go "off path". There will always be a tug back to the planned path, but no real punishment for this, as this is all part human spirits in our learning during life. Although, we'll often feel lost if we are off the path.

It's a common feeling with all humans, once off the chosen path. He further explained how this was all planned by ME. All so-called punishments for not staying on path were done by ourselves, humans tend to beat up themselves for notions we've strayed.

He then kinda dropped a bomb on me. I was tasked now to assist others in waking up. I had to teach others to take control, get back to path, using my unique gifts.

My next question was - "Wooo, okay, why me?"

Hermes just grinned.

As part of this waking up task, I am offering several things via my websites. I can help you wake up as well, by my books, or in the future, my movies or TV shows. (Links to my services are in the About The Author bit, plus Facebook Groups)

The ancient gods, who are advanced human souls in reality, want us to discover them again. They wish to show us how to use our own innate magik talents to expand, taking control of their lives for the first time. Stop ceding your life's path to others, take control, explore outwards, connect with the source of creation at the center of our universe, discover the multitude of dimensions where other spirits live, love, and play.

Push aside all the trappings taught to us by our religious overlords, and take for yourself the mantle of master of your own life, finally. Grab the controls, switch off autopilot, and go where your soul wants to take you.

Brief Overview of the Akashic Records

Picture a cosmic library, its shelves lined with the blueprints of every soul's journey—every thought, action, past life, future possibility—etched into an ethereal medium. This, my friends, is the Akashic Records. It's a concept that's been whispered through the annals of mystical tradition, a realm that grants its voyagers deep, sometimes unsettling, insights into the essence of existence.

But you won't be venturing alone. Imagine having Hermes—known also as Thoth in the Egyptian pantheon—as your personal guide. This ancient deity is not only the custodian of wisdom but also a celestial librarian, as it were, leading you through the labyrinthine corridors of Akasha. Hermes, with his perennial grin, will help you interpret, navigate, and make sense of this cosmic database. If you're like me, you'll come to cherish this spiritual companionship.

The goal here is triple-fold. First, we aim to unpack the concept of the Akashic Records. Second, we will delve into the practicalities of initiating contact with Hermes/Thoth, ensuring that your trip to the Records is both insightful and secure. And lastly, we'll focus on the actionable steps to harness this esoteric knowledge in your mundane life—be it in magick, personal growth, or mundane decision-making. You could say this book serves as your all-in-one travel guide and manual to the Akashic domain.

Whether you're a seasoned occultist, someone who's dabbled a bit in spiritualism, or a complete neophyte whose only experience with magick is Hollywood's glittery rendition, this book speaks to you. Each chapter builds upon the next, providing both a solid foundation for newcomers and challenging insights for the well-versed. And let's be honest, who wouldn't want a personal tour guide to the Akashic Records, especially when it's Hermes himself?

So, strap in, switch off that autopilot, and get ready for an unforgettable journey through the corridors of cosmic wisdom. As Hermes once told me with a grin, "Why you?" Well, once you turn that last page, you'll be saying, "Why not me?"

CHAPTER TWO

Defining the Akashic Records

So, what exactly are these things, these Akashic Records?

Imagine you're stepping into the world's most magnificent library, a place not made of bricks and mortar but of pure, shimmering consciousness. No book here is mundane; every volume is a unique universe unto itself, housing information about souls, events, thoughts, and potentialities. The air is electric, buzzing with the whispers of ages long past and epochs yet to come. What you're stepping into, dear seeker, is not a figment of fiction but the very real, pulsating essence of the Akashic Records.

The Akashic Records are often misconceived as a literal library, with leather-bound books and ancient scrolls. While that's a useful metaphor, it's just the tip of the iceberg. They're a multi-dimensional space where all knowledge—past, present, and potential future—is stored. Think of it as the spiritual internet: infinitely expansive, and yet, deeply personal. It's not your Sunday afternoon library; it's more like the Universe's cloud storage, holding a backup of the soul's journey across lifetimes.

Inside this spectacular etheric database, knowledge is divided into layers. There's the 'life layer,' containing details of your current existence. Then, deeper, the 'soul layer,' which goes back to when your spirit first sparked into being. Just like the different layers of Earth—from the crust down to the core—each layer here serves a purpose, catering to your spiritual queries at varying depths. Imagine peeling an onion where each layer reveals a deeper cosmic truth, and you've barely scratched the surface.

Now, who keeps this information safe and sound? Picture a librarian who's not limited by human faculties but is an archetypal, timeless entity. In various traditions, they are called the Record Keepers or Guardians. They're not gatekeepers, but guides, eager to help you navigate this cosmic repository. Imagine Gandalf and Dumbledore rolled into one, but multiply that wisdom by infinity—that's your cosmic librarian.

Remember, the Akashic Records are not a 'cheat sheet' for life. They won't tell you next week's lottery numbers or how to sidestep challenges. It's not about shortcuts; it's about soul-cuts—deep incisions that enable you to examine your spiritual fiber. Just like an art museum won't make you a painter, the Akashic Records won't turn you into a prophet. They offer tools, inspiration, and vistas of inner knowing, inviting you to become the alchemist of your destiny.

The Records are not a stagnant pool of data; they are dynamic and ever-changing. Every thought, decision, and action modifies your 'record,' much like editing a never-ending manuscript. Imagine Wikipedia, where articles are updated in real-time, except here, the content updates are more profound, affecting not just your life but the fabric of the Universe itself.

How to Think About It: The Metaphor of Light

You can think of the Akashic Records as light—both particle and wave. When focused upon, they solidify into 'particles'—concrete bits of knowledge or guidance. Left alone, they remain a 'wave,' an unmanifested potential of what you might discover. Like the famous double-slit experiment in quantum physics, your intent collapses the wave into particles, making abstract wisdom palpable. I don't plan to bore you with a discussion of quantum physics, although I took classes in this during my college years, a lot has changed. It's only gotten weirder. And if any of my old professors are still alive, they'd be tracking me down, armed with pitchforks for my writing such a book as this!

Access and Permission

Not everyone can saunter into the Pentagon and ask for state secrets. Similarly, there are protocols for entering this ethereal domain. Your heart's purity and intent are your security clearance. You can't pry into someone else's Records without explicit soul-level permission, making it a sacrosanct, and deeply ethical, undertaking. It's a spiritual equivalent of your fingerprint or retina scan, granting access only when there's a harmonic match.

I have done multiple readings, thus getting that permission, and revealing what I am allowed to reveal to the client. Sometimes I see a scroll, sometimes a heavy book, a tome. I rarely see what I was shown about my own records, a clear crystal block. Maybe I'm special. Well, at least my granny (maysherestinpeace) thought I was special.

I feel that being able to at least see your own records can assist you in correcting your path,

While the Akashic Records can bring revelation, they can also unearth deep-seated wounds and traumas. It's not a whimsical spiritual escapade, but a serious journey inward. It's like stepping into a chamber of mirrors, reflecting not just your light but also your shadow. So, the voyage needs to be approached with a sense of reverence and preparedness.

Finally, why should you care about the Akashic Records? Because they offer you the rarest commodity in our fast-paced world—self-understanding. This isn't merely about unlocking secrets of a past life as a pharaoh or a healer, though that's undeniably fascinating. It's about comprehending the core essence of your being, the indivisible spiritual DNA that makes you, you. It's like a cosmic interview where the subject and the journalist are the same—you, probing into the depths of your own soul, guided by the wisdom of ages.

As we lift the veil further, remember that you're not just a passive observer in this story; you're a dynamic participant, each step offering you tools to craft your own destiny. So, dear seeker, hold onto your proverbial hat, because we're about to journey from theoretical frameworks to practicalities, going deeper into the layered cake that is the Akashic Records—a voyage led by none other than the mythical Hermes, the custodian of cosmic secrets.

Historical Background and Literature

Have you ever wondered how the idea of a cosmic repository, like the Akashic Records, came to be? How did ancient mystics, scholars, and even civilizations separated by oceans arrive at a strikingly similar concept? Buckle up, fellow seeker, because we are about to embark on a whirlwind tour through time, spanning continents, faiths, and intellectual currents to unveil the historical tapestry that gives the Akashic Records their current shape and understanding.

The very term "Akashic" is derived from "Akasha," a Sanskrit word that means sky or ether. The ancient Vedas of India, scriptures dating back 5,000 years, were perhaps the first to introduce this notion. Imagine Vedic sages, deep in meditation beside the Ganges, receiving streams of celestial information. They believed that Akasha was the elemental fabric of existence, holding the memory of the Universe. It's as if the sky above, as ancient as time, has been taking notes.

Fast-forward a few millennia and take a leap to ancient Egypt. Meet Hermes Trismegistus, often equated with the Egyptian god Thoth. He was a philosopher, sage, and allegedly, the author of the Emerald Tablet, a compact text that declared: "As above, so below." Hermes, much like those Vedic seers, felt that the Universe was an intricate web of correspondences. Imagine his revelation as a timeless tweet that ricocheted through the esoteric corridors of history, resonating with the same frequencies as the Akashic Records.

Jump ahead again, this time to the late 19th and early 20th centuries. Meet Helena Petrovna Blavatsky, Annie Besant, and C.W. Leadbeater, the key players in the Theosophical movement. They brought the term 'Akashic Records' into modern esoteric discourse. Think of them as the Steve Jobs and Bill Gates of spiritual technology, refurbishing ancient wisdom for contemporary appetites. The Theosophists portrayed the Records as a tool for personal evolution and cosmic understanding, much like an advanced cosmic operating system available to those who could 'hack' into it.

Next, let's make a pitstop in the early-to-mid 20th century to meet Edgar Cayce, the American psychic and healer. Cayce accessed what he called the "Book of Life," effectively the Akashic Records, to diagnose illnesses and offer life advice while in a trance state. Picture Cayce as a spiritual detective, solving cases by thumbing through the celestial files of his subjects, which were as real to him as dusty tomes in an old library.

The concept of a universal memory bank also features prominently in Western Occult traditions. From Kabbalistic lore to the teachings of the Hermetic Order of the Golden Dawn, you'll find references that echo the essence of the Akashic Records. It's as if the Records are the ultimate cryptographic puzzle, a mystical Enigma machine with its code scattered across the globe, waiting for seekers to piece it together.

Believe it or not, even indigenous cultures, far removed from Eastern mysticism or Western occultism, have their versions of the Akashic Records. Shamanic traditions often speak of the 'Spirit World' as a reservoir of knowledge and wisdom. Imagine a Native American shaman journeying into the spirit realm, not with a compass and map, but with drums, chants, and a heart full of questions. Their 'spirit world' is like a local server connected to the universal cloud that is the Akashic Records.

By this point, you must be wondering how all these traditions and ideas connect. Well, that's where comparative mysticism comes into play. Scholars like Mircea Eliade, Joseph Campbell, and Carl Jung have studied the common threads that run through diverse spiritual narratives. Think of them as cosmic archeologists, excavating the ruins of disparate belief systems to reveal the unified structure beneath—like revealing that all roads do indeed lead to Rome, or in this case, the Akashic Records.

Science, too, flirts with the Akashic paradigm, albeit using different nomenclature. Concepts like the Morphic Field proposed by Rupert Sheldrake or the Zero-Point Field in quantum physics offer a materialistic counterpart to the Akashic Records. Imagine scientists in lab coats peering into microscopes and realizing that at the tiniest levels, the universe behaves like a vast, interconnected network—almost like a physical mirror reflecting the metaphysical Akashic Records. It was this part that finally tipped me over to admitting my science education shouldn't conflict with my knowledge of esoteric or occult ideas. In fact, it's a technology and a science all its own.

Lastly, the idea of the Akashic Records hasn't escaped the realm of literature and popular culture. From movies, TV shows, to speculative fiction, these ethereal records have made their mark. They serve as an alluring narrative device, a celestial MacGuffin that characters seek. Yet, what's fascinating is how these fictional accounts often stimulate real interest, leading people to explore the actual spiritual dimensions. They are, in effect, bridges between the mundane and the mystical.

As we close this history-laden section, it's crucial to see it as not just a parade of facts but a tapestry of interconnected wisdom, as vibrant and intricate as a Persian rug. And just like a skilled weaver, our next step will pull another colorful thread into the mix as we delve into the objectives behind accessing the Akashic Records. Ah, but that's a tale brimming with intentions, pitfalls, and boundless possibilities—subjects so compelling they could fill volumes, or perhaps even Records, of their own.

The Objectives of Accessing the Records

So, you've journeyed with me through ancient scriptures, met some of the seminal minds in modern esoteric thought, and even dabbled in the scientific paradigms that flirt with our subject. But all of this leaves one burning question: why would one want to access the Akashic Records? What's the point of flipping through a cosmic book if you're not going

15

to gain something meaningful from it?

We all have questions about ourselves that simple introspection or even extensive psychotherapy can't answer. The Akashic Records offer a sort of "soul-level" X-ray vision, allowing you to perceive the deeper mechanisms of your spiritual DNA. Imagine this as akin to looking at your genome but for your soul, revealing why you possess certain traits and not others, why specific experiences keep recurring, and why you feel a certain way around certain people. It's like finding an ancient manuscript that holds the secrets to your most puzzling life questions.

Revisiting past lives is not merely an esoteric exercise but a practical way to heal and understand present-life challenges. Perhaps you've felt that you're carrying a weight from another lifetime or that certain patterns feel inexplicably familiar. These Records allow you to address past karmas, as if they are a sort of spiritual ledger recording debits and credits from all your lifetimes. Imagine sorting through a dusty old attic and stumbling upon old letters that suddenly explain the present dynamics of your relationships.

What if you have dormant abilities that you're unaware of? Many believe that the Akashic Records can help unlock these latent talents. Suppose you always felt drawn to music but never pursued it. Maybe in another life, you were a composer, and those abilities lie latent within you. It's like having a treasure chest in your backyard but lacking the key or the map. The Akashic Records offer you both, empowering you to unearth talents buried deep within your soul. While I was sidelined by a medical issue in September 2022, I visited the records with Hermes, (BTW: this trip was the basis for this book!) I saw that I could access some talents from duplicate versions of my life this time, and one was painting. I'd tried to paint as a kid, but only now can I create works I consider to be actually good! A talent I accessed while on this trip to the Hall of Records.

It's said that while the Akashic Records contain the past and the present, they also include possible future trajectories. It's akin to navigating through a maze with a birds-eye view. You can see which paths lead to dead-ends and which ones bring you to the treasure. Accessing the Records can offer you unparalleled insight into the decisions that would be most harmonious with your soul's journey. Think of it as having a cosmic GPS that reroutes you whenever you take a wrong turn.

If spiritual enlightenment is your ultimate goal, the Akashic Records serve as an invaluable resource, a sort of divine library where you can learn the metaphysical laws of the universe. It's like being given a backstage pass to the cosmic theater, where you not only see how the 'magic tricks' are performed but also learn the underlying principles behind them. Your understanding moves from theory to experience, facilitating a quantum leap in your spiritual growth.

We are social beings, and relationships often present our most challenging and rewarding experiences. Accessing the Akashic Records can provide insights into soul contracts and karmic bonds, helping you understand the underlying dynamics of your relationships. It's like watching a film reel of your shared histories, offering explanations and insights that can transform relational discord into harmony.

Physical ailments often have energetic and spiritual roots. By delving into your Akashic Records, you might gain insights into the deeper causes of health issues. Imagine having a spiritual scalpel that could excise energetic blockages long before they manifest as physical diseases. Your visit to this ethereal realm could be a preventative trip to an otherworldly, holistic health clinic. Writing this bit reminded me I need to go back and continue to address the medical issues from 2022.

Creativity often comes from an elusive source. Many artists, writers, and musicians feel as if they channel their work from a realm beyond the ordinary senses. The Akashic Records can serve as this limitless muse. Picture tapping into an endless flow of divine inspiration, like a painter forever supplied with colors that never fade and a canvas that never ends.

You see, the objectives behind accessing the Akashic Records are as multifaceted as a finely cut gemstone, reflecting various hues depending on the angle of your inquiry. While some look for answers to personal questions, others may want to unravel the mysteries of existence itself. And then, there are those who are just curious, and oh, how the Akashic Records love curiosity. It's an invitation, a golden ticket to a cosmic carnival where every attraction holds the promise of deeper understanding and boundless wonder.

But understanding why one would want to venture into the Records naturally leads us to another crucial point: what are the theoretical frameworks that surround this ancient yet ever-renewed concept? For that, we must delve into the philosophies, the metaphysics, and even the contentious debates that surround the Akashic Records.

Ah yes, even celestial libraries have their controversies. But more on that later; for now, let your mind marinate in the myriad objectives we've explored. Trust me, we're just getting started.

Theoretical Frameworks Surrounding Akasha

If the Akashic Records are a celestial library, then its theoretical frameworks are the blueprints—detailing the architectural finesse that transforms it from an abstract imagination into a palpable reality. However, as with any blueprint, there are different interpretations and variations. And just like any avant-garde art piece or contentious scientific theory, the Akashic Records also provoke divergent views and heated debates.

In Eastern Philosophy, especially within the Vedic tradition, Akasha is considered the fifth element, a sort of ethereal matter that fills and surrounds the universe. It's not just empty space but is teeming with vibrational energy. Imagine, if you will, an ocean made not of water, but of pure potentiality—every ripple, every wave, an event or a thought or a possible future. In this ocean, you're not merely a swimmer but also a creator of ripples.

In the West, the idea of Akasha was popularized by the Theosophical Society, founded by Madame Helena Blavatsky. To these mystical thinkers, the Akashic Records were akin to an otherworldly Dewey Decimal System—a meticulously organized index of all knowledge, past, present, and possible future. It's as if they envisioned the Library of Alexandria, not as it was—limited and ultimately destructible—but as it could be: infinite and enduring.

Science, too, has touched upon concepts that mirror the idea of the Akashic Records. Some, not all, but some quantum physicists propose that we live in a holographic universe, where every part contains information about the whole. Imagine this: every cell in your body carrying the blueprint for the entire organism. In the same vein, each moment, each thought, and each action are imprinted into this cosmic hologram, accessible through the quantum field. I've seen some papers on this (I DO have a science degree, you know) and I can see their point; they make a credible argument. This ties in with the concept of Micro mirrors Macro, or the "As Above, So Below" concept.

In various religious traditions like Christianity and Judaism, there is mention of the "Book of Life," a record of the deeds of humanity, hinting at a concept not too dissimilar to the Akashic Records. It's as though each religion glimpsed a particular aisle in the grand cosmic library, but interpreted it through their own theological lens.

The New Age movement has popularized the Akashic Records as accessible through channeling and psychic intuition. Think of it as having your own personal librarian guiding you through a labyrinthine library. The Records are no longer distant or esoteric but have been democratized, made accessible to anyone willing to attune themselves to this higher frequency.

Carl Jung, the eminent Swiss psychiatrist, spoke of the "Collective Unconscious," a reservoir of experiences and archetypes shared by humanity. What if this was yet another aisle in the Akashic library? An aisle not just of personal experiences but of collective myths, stories, and lessons that have repeated throughout history. Imagine digging through not just your past, but humanity's past—learning not just from your experiences but from every human who has ever lived.

When dealing with a record of all events and emotions,

ethical considerations naturally arise. Accessing the Akashic Records isn't merely a matter of curiosity, but carries karmic responsibilities. Imagine finding a private diary in a public library. Even if it's available, should you read it? The Records challenge us to approach them with a sense of reverence and ethical integrity. Although I hesitate to use the word "karmic" here, but it's one of the naturals of our creation/universe. It's open to interpretation, and everyone seems to have their own ideas of what "karmic" actually means. Here's a fun experiment to run, go into any magik or new age social group and post a question about karma, and then sit back and watch the fireworks. I'm not encouraging you to be a troll, however the resulting arguments will begin to remind one of the Monty Python Argument Clinic sketch.

The latest framework to emerge emphasizes the transformative potential of the Akashic Records. No longer just a depository of information, the Records are a tool for profound personal transformation and healing. It's as if this cosmic library also contains a pharmacy, offering not just information but also the elixirs to transmute that knowledge into wisdom and healing.

And then there are the skeptics. I know they exist, and I have had "discussions" with a few. They argue that the Akashic Records are a fantastical invention, a comforting fairy tale for those seeking meaning. But even within skepticism, there's value. For, if we're to understand something as grand and elusive as the Akashic Records, it's important to consider all perspectives. Imagine a panel discussion where both fans and critics of a famous author are present. Isn't the understanding richer when it's well-rounded?

There you have it—a tour through the complex, multifaceted world of theories surrounding Akasha. We've navigated through ancient Eastern philosophies, Western esoteric traditions, modern scientific conjectures, and even touched upon ethical considerations. Now, as we've explored the 'why' and the 'what,' we are better equipped to dive into the 'how.' How does one prepare for this profound spiritual journey? Is there a roadmap, or do we create the path as we walk it? Ah, but let's not get ahead of ourselves. Each question, in its own time, brings forth its own set of wonders and revelations. And as you'll soon discover, the universe loves a curious mind.

Preparatory Steps for Akashic Exploration

So, there you are, you're standing on the precipice, gazing at the limitless horizon of Akashic knowledge. The air is charged with anticipation. But before we take that exhilarating leap into the abyss of cosmic wisdom, we must first prepare. Just as a mountaineer doesn't ascend Everest without meticulous planning, or a diver doesn't plunge into the ocean depths without adequate gear, one must be aptly prepared for Akashic exploration.

Understanding Intent: The Spiritual Compass

Before diving into any metaphysical journey, intent acts as your spiritual compass. Remember, the Akashic Records are not a circus or a funhouse; they are sacred space. Ask yourself, what is it that you seek? Enlightenment? Healing? Knowledge? Be as specific as you can. Your intent is your spiritual GPS, guiding you through the labyrinthine corridors of the Records. It sets the boundaries, narrows the scope, and enlightens the path ahead.

Emotional and Mental Cleansing: The Inner Purification

Let's shift our focus inwards for a moment. Think of yourself as a goblet, and the Akashic knowledge as wine. Would you pour exquisite wine into a dirty glass? Of course not! Similarly, Akashic wisdom flows best into a pure vessel. Practices like meditation, grounding, and energy cleansing rituals are not just preparatory steps; they're your first experience of Akashic energy—gentle ripples before the tidal wave.

Ethical Guidelines: The Sacred Vows

Earlier, we delved into the karmic laws and ethics associated with accessing the Akashic Records. Now, it's time to put those principles into action. Just like a hiker follows trail guidelines, you must adhere to certain ethical tenets. These can vary but often involve vows of confidentiality, integrity, and respect for the higher will. This isn't merely spiritual bureaucracy; it's setting the terms for a soul contract you're about to enter.

Building A Ritual Space: Your Akashic Altar

An athlete has a gym, a writer has a desk, and you, aspiring Akashic explorer, need a ritual space. This can be as elaborate as an altar adorned with crystals, candles, and sacred geometry, or as simple as a cushion in a quiet room. What matters is that it's a place where you can transition from the earthly to the ethereal. You're creating a portal, a cosmic gateway that resonates with your unique energy signature.

Selecting Tools and Symbols: The Cosmic Toolkit

Sacred tools can act as conductors, amplifying your natural psychic abilities and tuning you into the Akashic frequency. Think of them as tuning forks. When struck, they resonate at a specific vibration that aligns with the Records. Crystals like amethyst for higher consciousness or quartz for clarity can be excellent allies. Symbols and sigils may also be incorporated, serving as mnemonic devices or ethereal road signs.

Meditation and Visualization: The Mind's Voyage

This is where we rehearse the mind for its impending journey. Meditation and visualization techniques help you attune your consciousness to the frequencies of the Akashic realm. It's akin to acclimating to high altitudes before a mountaineering expedition. Through visualization, you may also construct an Akashic sanctuary—a mental construct that serves as your safe haven and point of access to the Records. I have a wonderful guided meditation, where I guide you through the process of lifting into a higher state of mind, the state where we can access our higher selves. I assist you in creating a safe haven, or workshop, from which to explore metaphysical and psychic worlds.

Seeking Guidance: Mentors, Guides, and Teachers

Sometimes, the path to the Akashic Records is not a solitary journey. Just as a ship has its captain and crew, you may benefit from guidance. Whether it's a physical mentor, a spiritual entity, or your own Higher Self, their wisdom can serve as beacons, especially when navigating through complex or emotionally charged information. Keep an open mind, but also exercise discernment. Not every guide offers the same quality of navigation.

Record-Keeping: The Akashic Journal

As a pioneering Akashic explorer, you're not just a consumer of wisdom but also its chronicler. Maintaining an Akashic journal serves a dual purpose. It not only documents your experiences but also aids in processing them. After all, the Akashic Records aren't just a treasure chest to be looted and forgotten. They are a living library, and each entry you make contributes to this ever-evolving database.

Closing Rituals: Sealing the Portal

When one embarks on a journey, there's often a farewell—a closing ritual that marks the end of one chapter and the beginning of reflection. The closing ritual is more than mere formality; it's a sealing of the portal, a polite goodbye, and a reintegration of the ethereal experiences into your physical reality.

And there we are, each step a crucial milestone on your upcoming expedition into the Akashic Records. As we wrap up these preparatory strategies, our souls are no longer standing at the precipice; we're soaring—each of us equipped with the knowledge, the wisdom, and the intent to navigate this cosmic tapestry. What awaits us is not just a record of all that was and will be, but a mirror reflecting our most authentic selves. The journey to the Akashic Records is not just about exploring the universe; it's about rediscovering who you truly are. And for that, my friend, no preparation is too rigorous, no caution too excessive.

CHAPTER THREE

Hermes/Thoth: The Messenger and Mediator Between Realms

Imagine standing at the edge of a grand cosmic ocean, where waves of light and shadows dance in an eternal ballet. You might be wondering how to navigate such an overwhelming expanse. Well, that's where Hermes in the Greek tradition, or Thoth in the Egyptian realm, comes into play. Like a celestial lighthouse keeper, he helps souls navigate through the complexities of this cosmic ocean.

The Dual Identity of Hermes/Thoth: Hermes in Greek mythology and Thoth in Egyptian mythology are not just names; they symbolize a cosmic force, a mediator between the divine and mortal realms. Think of them as the cosmic postal service, delivering messages between gods and humans, but also as a wise counselor teaching us how to decode these messages.

Hermes/Thoth in Sacred Texts: If Hermes/Thoth were to have a LinkedIn profile, it would be packed with endorsements for wisdom, writing, and arithmetic from gods and mortals alike. They're cited in various religious and esoteric manuscripts— from Egyptian Book of the Dead to Hermetic Corpus— acting as a guide to mystics and scholars through the ages.

Philosophical Foundations: Many philosophical schools of thought, such as Neoplatonism and Hermeticism, owe a great deal to Hermes/Thoth. They stand at the cradle of what we now term as the 'Western Esoteric Tradition,' acting as an initiator into secrets that common folks might term 'occult.'

The Conduit of Divine Wisdom: Imagine if divine wisdom was a stream of pure, crystal-clear water. In that case, Hermes/Thoth is the aqueduct channeling that wisdom into comprehensible ideas for humans, enabling us to sip from this cosmic stream without being overwhelmed.

Role in Alchemy and Astrology: It's no coincidence that both Hermes and Thoth are associated with the art of alchemy and the science of astrology. They act as patrons of these esoteric disciplines, guiding practitioners through the maze of symbols and metaphors towards enlightenment.

The Keeper of Boundaries and Transitions: Every threshold you cross, whether physical like doorways, or metaphorical like life stages, you'll find the trace of Hermes/Thoth. As the god of travelers and boundaries, he governs all sorts of transitions in the mortal and immortal worlds.

The story of Hermes/Thoth is not one to rush through. Picture yourself in an ancient library, its walls adorned with intricate hieroglyphics and celestial diagrams. The musty smell of parchment fills the air. As you pick up an aged scroll, you realize it's a text dedicated to Hermes/Thoth. Your heart pounds with anticipation. You're not just reading; you're engaging in a dialogue that stretches back millennia.

Now, let's delve into how these revered figures are presented in sacred texts, for therein lies the root of much of our understanding. Each manuscript adds another layer to this complex deity, inviting you to peep through the veils separating the mortal from the divine...

As you read on, the thought strikes you: This is not mere mythology; it's a sacred narrative pointing to truths just beyond the grasp of conventional wisdom. Ah, the thrill of esoteric discovery!

The Emerald Tablets: The Ancient Blueprint to Unlocking Cosmic Mysteries

The Provenance of the Emerald Tablets: The Story Behind The Sage

Think about being in a dusty library that hasn't seen visitors in years, its air heavy with the aroma of antiquity. Your fingers graze the cracked spines of long-forgotten books until they rest on an emerald-hued tome. A sense of awe fills you as you open the cover to reveal writings said to have originated from Thoth himself. "Ah," you might think, "what treasures of cosmic wisdom am I to discover within these pages?"

The Emerald Tablets are not just pieces of text but sacred relics imbued with the wisdom of Thoth, who was a central figure in Egyptian mythology. Ascribed to the ibis-headed god of wisdom, the Tablets are akin to an enigmatic treasure map, offering tantalizing glimpses into the very fabric of existence. The words engraved on the tablets hold a dual purpose: as historical anecdotes and as metaphysical pointers guiding the curious souls toward realms unfathomable. By understanding the origins of these Tablets, you're not just reading; you're engaging in an archaeological dig into the psyche of the ancient world, dusting off millennia of misconceptions to reveal the shining gems of timeless wisdom beneath.

The Wisdom Encoded: A Cryptic Encyclopedia for the Cosmic Explorer

Let's imagine the Tablets as a kind of celestial GPS, one that could guide you through the maze-like intricacies of the universe, including the mystical Akashic Records. You're not just viewing a map; you're looking at the coding language of the universe itself, encrypted messages waiting to be deciphered. Picture a cosmic scavenger hunt where each line of the text acts like a cipher, unlocking specific coordinates to various corners of the cosmos.

Much like a musical composition, the wisdom in the Tablets is layered and complex, yet harmonious. The texts are filled with philosophical, scientific, and spiritual concepts entwined in a web of symbology. Every syllable of this ancient language reverberates with multiple meanings, stretching from the concrete to the abstract, from the earthly to the heavenly. You can almost sense the glyphs rising from the pages to dance before your eyes, each character inviting you to a waltz of wisdom that spirals into greater and greater circles of understanding.

The Connection to Akashic Records: The Cosmic Ledger's Master Key

If the universe is a vast, expansive library, then the Akashic Records serve as the ledger that keeps track of every event, thought, and emotion experienced by every soul. Now, what if I told you the Emerald Tablets are the VIP pass granting you access to this celestial repository? Think of these Records as a high-security vault and the Emerald Tablets as the unique key that can crack the code.

The Tablets often speak in riddles and parables, dropping cryptic hints about the Akashic Records. They offer clues in the form of allegories, compelling you to look beyond literal meanings and understand the metaphoric language they employ. As you begin to comprehend the text, you may find your internal vision adjusting, much like your eyes adapting to a dark room. Slowly but surely, the fog lifts, revealing a dazzling landscape of celestial chronicles, the Akashic Records laid bare for your eyes to feast upon. And at that moment, the words of the Emerald Tablets, coded and elusive, will ring in your ears like a triumphant symphony, congratulating you on unlocking one of the universe's most jealously guarded secrets.

By now, you might be wondering, what could be so secretive yet so universally profound that a deity would go through the trouble of encrypting it into the very fabric of these Tablets? Ah, that's where our next exploration takes us, to delve deeper into how this ancient knowledge was preserved, lost, and once again unearthed to the seekers of truth.

Symbols and Rituals Linked to Hermes/Thoth: The Linguistic Keys and Ceremonial Doors to Wisdom

The Caduceus: A Mystical Staff Entwined with Cosmic DNA

Imagine walking through an ancient set of ruins where each column or building is a living glyph, an embodiment of cosmic principles. As you venture deeper into this mystical grove, you come upon a serpent-entwined staff gleaming in the soft light filtering through the canopy above. Ah, the Caduceus! Often mistaken for a medical symbol, this magical staff is Hermes' signature tool. The serpents symbolize the life force or Kundalini energy, weaving around the staff like a DNA helix.

At first glance, the Caduceus may seem like an intriguing piece of art, but in the hands of the initiate, it transforms into a wand of alchemy. The staff represents the axis mundi, a celestial pillar connecting Earth to the heavens, while the serpents symbolize duality—conscious and unconscious, physical and ethereal. Picture it as your spiritual antenna, boosting your metaphysical reception and sending out waves of intention across the cosmic web. When used in rituals, the Caduceus isn't just an accessory; it's a navigational tool that guides you through the multilayered tapestry of existence.

Rituals of Invocation: The Spoken Charms that Usher Divine Presence

Think of the words you speak in a ritual as the brushstrokes in an impressionist painting; individually, they may seem like dabs of color, but when executed in sequence, they reveal a masterful landscape of intention and will. Hermes/Thoth is particularly fond of linguistics; after all, he's credited with the invention of language. The rituals associated with him aren't mere recitations; they're poetic dialogues with the universe, a divine language coded in metaphor and rhythm.

Imagine standing within a sacred circle, chanting hymns and invocations that trace their lineage back to ancient Egyptian temples and Grecian groves. As you intone these mystical phrases, envision shimmering glyphs forming in the air around you, as if your voice is painting with light. Each utterance is a key turning a lock within the ether, gradually opening the celestial gate that allows the energy of Hermes/Thoth to flow through. You're not merely speaking; you're weaving a tapestry of sound and intention that serves as an astral passport, stamped and approved by Hermes/Thoth himself.

Sacred Geometry and Alphabets: The Cosmic Code Behind Physical Reality

Now, have you ever wondered how the world might look if you could see the underlying geometry of existence? Imagine walking through life with a pair of magical glasses that reveal the matrix of lines, shapes, and angles orchestrating the dance of matter and energy. That's what engaging with the sacred geometry and alphabets linked to Hermes/Thoth feels like.

These are not mere shapes or letters but condensed packets of information, the DNA of the cosmos crystallized into understandable forms. When incorporated into rituals or meditative practices, these symbols act like tuning forks, resonating with particular frequencies within the great cosmic symphony. They become active participants in the ritual, inviting you to experience a harmonious blend of matter and spirit.

By this point, you might feel like an astral cartographer, tracing the invisible routes that connect symbols to gods and rituals to cosmic events. You're piecing together a cosmic puzzle, a grand tapestry where every thread is woven with intention and every knot is a nexus of infinite possibilities. And just when you think you've unraveled all there is to know, you discover another layer of complexity, a deeper level of understanding, enticing you to explore further into the labyrinthine cosmos guided by Hermes/Thoth.

The Role of Hermes/Thoth as a Gatekeeper to the Akashic Records

Picture this—you find yourself in an otherworldly library, where every book is a luminescent tablet that holds the sum of all knowledge across time and space. This is the Akashic Records, and standing at the entrance is none other than Hermes/Thoth, holding a golden key. He is your librarian, your guide, and the curator of these celestial archives.

When you hear the term "Akashic Records," think of it as the universe's hard drive. It contains the script of every moment, from the tiniest ripple in a pond to the cataclysmic death of stars. Hermes/Thoth, in his role as the master of wisdom, is the one who can grant you access to this forbidden vault of knowledge. He's not just a figurehead; he's an active participant in your quest, advising you on how to navigate the layers of information and revealing to you the mysterious syntax by which these records can be read and understood.

The Esoteric Techniques Taught by Hermes/Thoth for

Accessing Akashic Wisdom

The notion of accessing the Akashic Records might appear as fantastical as flapping your arms and flying across the country, but rest assured, there's a method to this mystical endeavor. And who better to teach these esoteric techniques than Hermes/Thoth himself?

You might think of these techniques as spiritual algorithms, a sequence of ritualistic steps that decode the invisible patterns woven into the fabric of reality. These could include advanced meditations, astral projections, and even mantra-like incantations that resonate on frequencies capable of vibrating the very locks off the gates to the Akashic Records. When practicing these techniques, you'll often find Hermes/Thoth there beside you in astral form, almost as though he's a spiritual mentor guiding your hand as you turn the pages of this celestial manuscript. You're not just opening a book; you're opening a doorway to infinite wisdom, a threshold only crossed under the watchful eye of Hermes/Thoth.

The Ethical Considerations and Karmic Implications

As intriguing as it is to tap into an all-encompassing source of cosmic knowledge, there are ethical and karmic considerations you should ponder before embarking on such a journey. Picture the Akashic Records as the universe's most sensitive diary. Would you open someone's diary without permission? Certainly not. And you would be wise to approach the Akashic Records with the same reverence and ethical mindfulness.

Hermes/Thoth, ever the balanced deity of wisdom and ethics, will ensure you don't misuse this privilege. Any attempt to exploit the Akashic Records for nefarious purposes won't just close the door, but could result in karmic consequences that reverberate across lifetimes. Your ethical standing with Hermes/Thoth and the Akashic Records themselves serves as a kind of metaphysical credit score, determining the level of access you're granted. Be mindful, respectful, and above all, worthy.

At this stage, you're standing at the precipice of esoteric discovery, peering into a world of limitless understanding and timeless wisdom. With the guidance of Hermes/Thoth, you're not just a wanderer; you're an explorer, mapping out territories in realms most dare not even dream of. Each layer of knowledge peeled back is another veil removed from the face of reality itself, and Hermes/Thoth stands beside you, key in hand, ready to unlock the next door. So take a deep breath, embrace the enormity of the moment, and step into the labyrinthine halls of cosmic wisdom. The adventure is just beginning.

The Duality of Hermes/Thoth: The Cosmic Guide Who Also Guards the Gates

The Janus-Faced Nature of Hermes/Thoth: Protector and Pathfinder

Imagine being lost in a dense forest, the sky veiled by a

canopy of leaves, your compass hopelessly spinning in circles. Out of the shadows steps a figure holding a lantern in one hand and a shield in the other. This figure is Hermes/Thoth, the deity who is as much your guide through the tangle of esoteric mysteries as he is the protector of those very secrets you seek.

His lantern illuminates your path, offering wisdom where there's ignorance and showing you how to sidestep pitfalls you'd never see coming. However, the shield he holds is not for you— it's to protect the sacred truths from being misused or desecrated. Hermes/Thoth is that sublime paradox: the librarian who will help you find the book you seek, but also the sentinel who ensures you're worthy of reading its contents in the first place.

Just like a prism disperses a single beam of light into its various spectral components, Hermes/Thoth embodies multifaceted roles that may seem contradictory but are harmoniously unified in him. Understanding this duality is key to approaching Hermes/Thoth in the correct manner, respecting both his guiding and guarding aspects, as you would respect both the inviting glow and the searing heat of a campfire.

The Dynamic Balancing Act: How Hermes/Thoth Chooses Who to Guide and Who to Guard Against

Have you ever played a complex game, where the rules constantly change and what helps you one moment might hinder you the next? Think of your interaction with Hermes/Thoth as just that—a dynamic balancing act where your actions, intentions, and even your very essence are constantly weighed and measured.

Just as a wise elder in a village might carefully evaluate who is permitted to handle a potent artifact, Hermes/Thoth assesses the spiritual maturity, intent, and readiness of the seeker. Sometimes, it might be a riddle you must solve, an esoteric insight you have to gain, or a moral challenge you need to overcome. It's a never-ending dance where you must keep pace with the tempo set by Hermes/Thoth, realizing that while he might extend his hand to guide you one moment, he won't hesitate to activate an impenetrable barrier if you falter or reveal unscrupulous intent.

Let's say you've gained a certain level of spiritual wisdom and esoteric understanding—congratulations, you're now a privileged guest at a celestial gala! But beware; just as one ill-advised comment can turn you from the guest of honor into a social pariah, a single misstep in your esoteric practices can also change Hermes/Thoth's role from a guide to a gatekeeper who shuts you out from further knowledge.

Wisdom and Discretion: The Two Pillars of Hermes/Thoth's Dual Role

Now, you might be wondering, "If Hermes/Thoth plays both sides, how can I ever hope to navigate this labyrinth of spiritual truths and metaphysical mysteries?" Ah, dear seeker, that's where wisdom and discretion come in. These are the currencies by which Hermes/Thoth deals—two pillars holding up the gate to the esoteric realm.

Wisdom isn't just about gathering information; it's about the application and synthesis of that knowledge into transformative life principles. On the other hand, discretion ensures that you approach the sacred mysteries with the respect and restraint they deserve. It's the whisper in your ear that tells you when to speak and when to remain silent, when to act, and when to withdraw.

When you possess both, you'll find that Hermes/Thoth becomes a benevolent guide, sharing arcane secrets like a magician, revealing the tricks of his trade to a cherished apprentice. Fail to honor these principles, and he becomes the stern guardian, holding his shield high, protecting the sanctity of the very mysteries you seek.

From this point, you're beginning to see Hermes/Thoth not just as an abstract concept or a remote deity, but as an active, multidimensional force in your spiritual journey. He's that indefinable essence that challenges you, guides you, shields you, and, most importantly, transforms you. Your next step? Embrace this duality. Embrace the contradiction, the paradox, and the mystery. For in doing so, you won't just find Hermes/Thoth— you'll find yourself.

Pathworking Ritual to prepare for the Journey

Here's a four-step pathworking ritual that blends traditional magical practices with your unique style. This ritual is best performed in a quiet, sacred space where you won't be disturbed.

Step 1: Prepare Your Sacred Space

What You'll Need:

- A piece of paper and a pen
- A feather to represent Hermes
- A candle (preferably orange or yellow)
- Incense (cedarwood or lavender work well)

Actions:

Light the candle and incense to prepare the space.

Write down your intention on the piece of paper, for example, "To seek guidance from Hermes for accessing the Akashic Records."

Place the feather next to the candle.

Key Point:

Physical items anchor your intent, making it more palpable and potent.

Step 2: Grounding and Centering

Actions:

Sit or stand comfortably.

Close your eyes and take deep, grounding breaths.

Envision roots extending from your feet deep into the Earth.

Draw the Earth's energy into your body with each inhale and release tension with each exhale.

Key Point:

Grounding is like fastening your cosmic seatbelt. You're preparing for take-off but ensuring a smooth landing.

Step 3: Invocation of Hermes

Actions:

Hold the feather and speak the following invocation:

"Hermes, Guide of Souls and Messenger Divine, I seek your wisdom and assistance."

Imagine Hermes appearing before you, perhaps as a young man with winged sandals or however you envision him.

Present your written intention to Hermes in your visualization. See him reading it and nodding.

Listen for any messages, symbols, or feelings that arise.

Key Point:

The invocation is your spiritual telephone call. The more clearly you voice your intentions, the stronger the connection.

Step 4: Close the Ritual and Journal

Actions:

Thank Hermes for his guidance and wisdom.

Extinguish the candle and incense.

Journal about your experience, taking note of any messages, symbols, or feelings.

Keep the feather and your written intention on your altar or a special place as a reminder of your quest.

Key Point:

After stepping out of the cosmic conversation, documentation serves as your post-ritual "voice memo." It helps capture what might otherwise evaporate in the mundane world.

This special action step should get you ready for what comes next.

CHAPTER FOUR

Preparations for the Journey: The Imperative of Physical Readiness

The Body as a Vessel: Navigating the Cosmic Oceans

Imagine being the master of an ancient seafaring ship, its wooden planks seasoned by the salt and sun, its sails filling with air like the lungs of some mythical sea creature. There you stand, facing an infinite horizon teeming with endless possibilities and shrouded in celestial mystery. However, to steer your vessel through both perilous and alluring waters, it must be in optimal condition. This ship is a metaphor for your own body, which carries your spirit through the grand odyssey of esoteric exploration.

Would you venture out into turbulent waters in a decrepit ship? Of course not. In the same manner, your body must be physically fit to navigate the complex matrix of mystical wisdom. Your physical health is a reflection of your commitment to spiritual exploration. Your body isn't merely a receptacle; it's a living sanctuary for the divine forces you're eager to understand.

Harmonizing the Physical and Spiritual: Body-Mind Synchronization

Recall the delicate act of fine-tuning an old radio, slowly adjusting the dial to find that elusive station. You wrestle with static, with scattered fragments of other signals, until at last—the crystal-clear sound of the sought-after melody fills the air. This fine-tuning is analogous to achieving equilibrium between your physical state and your spiritual aspirations.

Disciplines such as yoga, martial arts, or contemplative walking serve as more than mere exercises; they are bodily rituals, each movement a physical prayer designed to synchronize your earthly rhythms with celestial harmonies. Ignoring this crucial balance is like setting off on a treasure hunt without a compass—an incomplete endeavor. I often walk through the forest here, using it as a meditation walk and as a way to hang out in nature. Unlike back in Texas, here in New England, the trees tower over me as I walk, and I'm not as careful where I step, because, unlike Texas (or Australia for that matter) there are no venomous snakes here.

Your Body as a Living Lexicon: Imprinting Wisdom on Your Physical Self

Can you fathom the idea that your body might act as a living book of shadows, each cell a microscopic vessel containing traces of mystical insight? With each ritual and meditation practice, even through the foods you consume, you can inscribe this ancient wisdom into your very being.

Imagine each ritualistic gesture as a brushstroke painting your physical canvas, each focused breath as a note in your life's symphony. And the sustenance you consume? See it as the ink that fuels your bodily pen, allowing you to inscribe your soul's poetry onto your bodily parchment. Your well-being becomes not just a shield against disease, but a vessel capable of containing a living archive of mystical knowledge.

As we venture further into the heart of these mysteries, recognize that this path isn't simply a casual encounter with esoteric curiosities. It's a sacred pilgrimage demanding your whole being—body, mind, and soul. So prepare yourself diligently. Before you can tread the hallowed halls of mystical knowledge, your physical vessel must be shipshape for the voyage ahead. What would a captain be without a dependable ship? An explorer without the right equipment? When you attend to these physical preparations, you're not just getting ready for a journey; you're preparing for a spiritual expedition of a lifetime. And oh, the wonders that await!

Preparations for the Journey: Tuning the Emotional Frequencies

Your emotions are a dammed reservoir, full of potent, untapped energy. It's neither inherently good nor bad; it's what you make of it. Yet, just like water can either power a turbine or cause a flood, emotions can be an empowering force or an overwhelming deluge. The journey you're about to undertake—unfathomable, mysterious, and brimming with ancient wisdom—requires that you harness this reservoir, this emotional might, in the right way.

You must not treat your emotional state like an appendix, a throwaway part of you that has no purpose. Rather, see it as the heart of your esoteric journey. Through a repertoire of sacred practices—meditation, introspective journaling, or even ritualistic dancing—you're not just conditioning your body but calibrating your emotional core. Imagine feeling your emotional energies align with your intentions each time you inhale the scent of sacred incense or utter a spell. Incredibly, right?

I first knew I was psychic because I could pick up other people's emotions, and spirit will communicate using emotions. When I have you visualize while in a ritual, I advise you to also feel the emotions of your desire manifesting. Never underestimate the importance of your emotions.

Emotional Alchemy: Turning Doubt into Curiosity, Fear into Reverence

Think about an oyster transforming a grain of sand, an irritant, into a pearl—a gem of inestimable value. That's emotional alchemy. It's not about eliminating so-called 'negative' emotions; it's about transformation. Let's face it: esoteric paths are filled with elements that may induce doubt or even fear. Ghost stories aren't just tales told around campfires; they're cautionary narratives warning us about the consequences of ill-preparedness and disrespect toward hidden forces.

In this sense, fear and doubt are not your enemies. They're signals that your emotional compass is functioning. When you feel these stirrings, it's time to convert them into reverence and curiosity. Imagine transforming each twinge of doubt into a vibrant question mark, urging you to explore deeper mysteries. Feel that fear? Turn it into awe and respect, the way one might feel entering a sacred temple for the first time. There are no fears, only challenges; no doubts, only unfinished thoughts yearning for resolution.

The Symbiosis of Emotion and Intuition: Your Internal Compass

Ever walked into a room and sensed its mood without

anyone saying a word? That's intuition, the unsung hero that often complements our emotional states. Think of intuition as a deep-sea diver, fearlessly plumbing the depths of your subconscious to retrieve pearls of wisdom that might otherwise remain hidden. But this diver needs proper conditions to do his work—clear emotional waters.

Imagine your emotional states as varying weather conditions in your soul's landscape. Your intuitive abilities can either flourish like fauna in the springtime or wither away like leaves in harsh winter, depending on your emotional climate. Whether through focused meditation or trusted divination tools like Tarot, honing your intuition involves maintaining an emotional ecosystem conducive to growth and discovery.

You see, the emotional world is not separate from your spiritual quest; it's an integral part of it. A journeyman who is not emotionally prepared is like a cartographer without a map, a miner without a lantern. So, as you make your sacred preparations, remember that emotional readiness is not an optional accessory but essential gear for your mystical sojourn. And as we take our next steps into this profound and sometimes bewildering realm, consider this: the real treasure is not just the mystical wisdom you'll acquire but also the emotional intelligence and soulful intuition that will become your lifetime companions. The path is ready. Are you?

Preparations for the Journey: The Foundation of Intellectual

Rigor

The Library of the Mind: Cultivating a Garden of Knowledge

Imagine a grand library filled with leather-bound books, walls adorned with maps, and mahogany tables laden with ancient scrolls. This library is in your mind, and each book represents knowledge and wisdom you've accumulated over the years. In esoteric pursuits, the more expansive your library, the more profound your journey. You can think of intellectual grounding as cultivating this internal garden of knowledge. Reading works of ancient philosophers, keeping up with modern interpretations of arcane practices, and attending lectures only enrich the soil of your intellectual garden.

It's important to be familiar with the basic doctrines and philosophies underpinning your chosen mystical path. Like an experienced botanist who knows which plants require direct sunlight and which are best suited for the shade, knowing the foundational theories behind practices you are about to engage in will set you up for success. You won't just understand what you're doing; you'll grasp why you're doing it, which is equally crucial. That's right! We're transforming you into not just a mystical traveler, but a learned guide to your own journey.

Critical Thinking: The Guardian at the Gates

Imagine you're Indiana Jones in the third installment of his epic journey, at the chasm where he must choose the Holy Grail. Here, just like Indy, critical thinking is your guardian at the gates. Not everything that shines is gold, and not every mysterious path leads to enlightenment. Understanding this is crucial because your intellectual curiosity will serve as the guardian of your spiritual journey, separating the wheat from the chaff.

As you navigate through complex theories, encounter various spiritual entities, or interpret intricate symbols, your intellectual grounding will serve as your compass. By all means, believe in the ethereal and the fantastical, but also question them. A seeker of wisdom must be wise enough to question the wisdom presented to them. Embrace skepticism as a form of reverence for the truth, and you'll find that you're not dismissing opportunities for growth, but safeguarding the integrity of your quest.

Synergy of Intellect and Experience: The Alchemist's Crucible

In a lab filled with bubbling cauldrons and multi-colored vials, the alchemist doesn't merely toss in random elements hoping for gold; they follow specific principles. They understand that certain metals react in specific ways under particular conditions. Likewise, merging your intellectual understanding with real-world practices makes the journey itself the ultimate experiment in alchemy. The synergy between bookish knowledge and actual experiences becomes your crucible—a vessel where transformation occurs.

Imagine reading about an arcane ritual, aware of its historical context, the reasons for each symbol, and then performing it. The experience isn't just tactile but also profoundly meaningful because your intellectual groundwork magnifies the potency of your actions. You're not just chanting words; you're invoking age-old energies. You're not merely lighting candles; you're illuminating paths into shadowy realms of consciousness.

Such a synthesis of intellect and experience makes each step not just a move forward but a leap—a graceful arc that elevates your journey from mere exploration to profound discovery. You become not just a passerby, but a true citizen of this arcane landscape, fluent in its language, respectful of its customs, and most importantly, aware of its laws. What awaits you isn't just novelty, but nuanced understanding—a tapestry of wisdom woven from the golden threads of intellectual rigor and experiential enlightenment.

Ah, dear reader, as you see, intellectual grounding isn't a tedious task but an invigorating challenge. It's not just about absorbing information; it's about becoming a different, more complete version of yourself. A version that's ready for what lies ahead—equipped, enlightened, and ever-curious. So, shall we turn the page?

Assembling Your Magikal Toolkit: Embarking on a Mystical Adventure

The Importance of the Right Tools: Becoming a Mystical Craftsman

Just like with high Magik, where we use tools and props to craft and work magik rituals, or think about a master carpenter crafting a beautiful wooden cabinet. The care they take in choosing the right types of wood, the precise measurements they take, and the specialized tools they use are all part of the art form. Similarly, you, the seeker, are embarking on a mystical journey, and your magikal toolkit serves as your set of specialized tools. The items you include should not only be in line with your purpose, but should resonate with you on a deeply spiritual level. Crystals, herbs, wands, and amulets—each carries its own vibration, its own meaning.

You wouldn't try to hammer a nail with a screwdriver; likewise, you wouldn't use a piece of turquoise when you need the grounding qualities of hematite. As you select each item for your toolkit, ponder not only on its practical use but also on its symbolic resonance. Will it amplify your intentions or perhaps open doors to specific dimensions? When you strike a balance between function and symbolism, your toolkit becomes an extension of yourself—a collection of allies in physical form.

Creating Synergy: The Orchestra of Energies

Imagine an orchestra, where every instrument plays a unique but crucial role. The violin can sing a sweet melody, and the drum can set the rhythm, but it's their collaboration that creates a symphony. Your magikal toolkit is similar; each item has its own energy, its own voice. But when combined effectively, they form an ethereal orchestra that can play the symphony of your intentions.

Consider the energies you're bringing together. The incense might serve to purify the space, your athame to direct will, and your chosen gemstones could amplify energies. Make sure these items harmonize. Have you ever noticed how a drop of ink can change the color of an entire glass of water? A single discordant energy can alter the efficacy of your magikal workings. So, fine-tune your toolkit. Spend time with it. Meditate on the energies each item represents and think about how they can harmonize to create something truly powerful and unique to your journey.

The Living Toolkit: Evolving with Your Journey

Much like a painter's palette changes depending on the

scene they're painting, your toolkit will need to evolve. You might be tempted to find some essential items and consider your toolkit complete, but in truth, it should be as fluid and evolving as you are. Just as a martial artist learns new techniques to face different challenges, you must be willing to adapt your toolkit to suit new spiritual landscapes.

Picture a journey through a mysterious, ever-changing forest. You started in a sunlit meadow and found that a particular herb helped you connect with the elemental spirits there. But now, you're entering a dense, shadowy woodland. The same herb may not be as useful here; perhaps it's time to add a small lantern imbued with protective runes. This is the living toolkit: adaptable, evolving, and forever tuned to your needs.

Remember, you're not assembling a static box of trinkets but cultivating a living ecosystem of energies and intentions that grows with you. So don't rush it. Take your time to select, cleanse, and charge each item. Your toolkit is an intimate part of your mystical journey; treat it with the reverence and thoughtfulness it deserves.

So, do you feel the anticipation building up? Just as a master craftsman feels a sense of sacredness when selecting the wood for a new project, you should feel a similar thrill as you begin to assemble your magikal toolkit. This isn't just preparation; it's a rite of passage. A rite that says, "I am ready.

I am committed. Let the adventure begin." Shall we take the next step together?

Setting Clear and Specific Intentions: The Cartographer of Your Soul's Odyssey

The Compass of Desire: How Intention Sets Your Course

Imagine you're an explorer standing on the edge of an uncharted wilderness. Would you step forward without a map or a compass? Likely not. In the world of magik, your intentions act as both. A clear and focused intention is like calibrating your inner compass, aligning it with the universe's magnetic fields to guide you toward your true north. Intentions are the center of all magik, whether you do Law of Attraction, Chaos Magik, or full up High Magik Rituals: It's all about INTENT!

You may want to change your life, find love, or unlock spiritual wisdom. Whatever it is, the more precise you are, the better. Vagueness is the fog that confuses the compass. Say, for instance, you desire prosperity. Instead of merely focusing on "more money," visualize what prosperity looks like in detail. How does it feel to touch, smell, even taste that prosperity? That level of specificity fine-tunes your spiritual compass and allows you to set a course through the metaphysical wilderness with confidence.

The Magic of Syllables: Crafting Your Intention Statement

Now that you know where you're heading, you need a rallying cry, a set of magic words that encapsulate your goal— this is your intention statement. It's akin to a songwriter capturing an intricate emotion in a single lyric. The right words can send shivers down your spine or bring tears to your eyes. Similarly, your intention statement needs to be so on point that saying it makes you feel like you've already set the wheels of fate into motion.

Create an intention statement that's not only clear but also resonates with you emotionally. Avoid cliche phrases and go for words that stir your soul. Let it be simple but weighty, like a rune filled with ancestral wisdom. "I welcome love that nourishes my soul," for example, has a greater emotional heft than a mere "I want a good relationship." Such a carefully crafted statement vibrates with your inner truth, turning your words into a spell of extraordinary power.

An intention statement is what ALL magik starts out as - from chaos magik/sigil magik to High Magik. The statement is the core of it all. So, craft this carefully.

Being the Archer, Not the Arrow: Allowing Room for Divine Maneuver

Specific intentions are crucial, but there's a subtle art in leaving just enough room for the universe to work its magic. Imagine you're an archer: you aim carefully, pull the bowstring with just the right amount of tension, and let the arrow fly. Yet, once the arrow is in the air, it's out of your hands. Winds could shift, and other unseen forces come into play. This is where you need to allow room for divine maneuver.

While you should have a targeted intention, it's equally important to understand that the universe might have detours that are beyond human understanding. Trust that the cosmic forces are aligning in your favor, even if the path isn't straightforward. When you articulate your intention, append it with the wisdom of openness, like adding, "This or something better for my highest good." This not only confirms your goal but also welcomes the divine mystery, the unpredictable winds that might just carry your arrow to an even more magnificent destination.

Ah, the electric thrill of setting intentions! It's as if you're standing on a cliff overlooking a grand landscape, your spirit eager to soar over forests, rivers, and mountains. Yet, the sensation isn't born merely from the allure of what lies ahead; it springs from a newfound trust in yourself. You have your compass; you've inscribed your map. Feel that? It's not just the wind against your face; it's the future calling, a symphony of what's yet to come, waiting for your baton to set its music free.

We're about ready to begin the Astral Journey.

CHAPTER FIVE

Ritual Design for Invoking Hermes/Thoth: The Cosmic Theatre Where Gods Take the Stage

The Set Design: Crafting the Sacred Space

By now, many of you know I also write for film, and I also shoot short films when I can. I'm going to relate all that follows as if it's a huge production for a theater. Not a small off, off-Broadway theater, but the big theaters in New York, London, or Los Angeles.

Imagine a theater, the curtains yet to be raised, the stage awaiting the performers, each prop and backdrop in its perfect place. The stage manager drops his reading glasses into place. He's waiting for you. You see, this is your ritual space, awaiting the divine actor Hermes or Thoth. The beauty of ritual is akin to the artistry that turns a simple platform into a whole new world under the stage lights. A chalice, a wand, an altar—

these aren't mere objects but powerful symbols that the gods recognize as the language of your intention.

Begin by setting your stage—your sacred space. Each item you choose to include is a line in a poetic invitation to the gods. A feather for Thoth, the God of Wisdom, or perhaps a lyre for Hermes, the Messenger. Be thoughtful about your choices; these symbols serve as your script in this divine play. Like an actor memorizing each line, you should know the symbolism behind each object, for it tells a story that resonates in the otherworldly realms.

The Script: Arranging the Ritual Elements and Sequence

In any compelling theater production (or TV or film production), there is a script that actors follow—a story that unfolds in a carefully orchestrated sequence. This is true for your ritual as well; the order matters. Are you starting with an invocation or jumping straight into a chant? There's a rhythm, a cadence to the ritual, and each element builds upon the previous. Like a composer arranging notes into a symphony, you're arranging the elements of your ritual to evoke the qualities of Hermes or Thoth.

Begin with a grounding exercise, perhaps a visualization of roots growing from your feet into the earth, connecting you to the wisdom of the ancients. Then, as you call upon the god, use their mythos to guide the script. If Hermes is your divine guest, perhaps you might symbolize his fleet-footedness with a circle of feathers. If Thoth, the weight of wisdom might be represented by a scale, balanced perfectly. Like a compelling narrative twist, let each phase of your ritual surprise and delight the deity, inviting them further and further into your circle.

The Performance: Harmonizing Your Energy with the Divine

Ah, the climax! The moment the actor delivers the monologue that leaves the audience in tears, or the grand reveal that flips the story on its head. In a ritual, this peak moment is your personal interaction with Hermes or Thoth. And just like the best performers exude a natural aura that captivates their audience, your energy must be in harmony with the deity you're invoking. This isn't a time for hesitation; it's your solo under the spotlight.

Raise your energy to meet theirs. Visualize the deity stepping into your circle, hearing your invitation, and sitting down to a cosmic tête-à-tête with you. Whether you choose to engage in divination, channeling, or simply sitting in their divine presence, this is the moment to lean into the encounter fully. Your energy, focused and elevated, serves as the encore that seals the ritual and leaves an impression on the divine.

And then, as the curtain falls, and the audience—both earthly and divine—erupts in applause, you'll realize that the stage was never just a platform, but a bridge between worlds. A bridge that you built, using symbols as bricks and your intention as the mortar. The deity departs, but the resonance lingers, like the haunting notes of a melody long after the music has stopped.

Do you feel it? The charged air, the almost-audible whispers of divine laughter, the warmth of an ethereal embrace? If so, you've successfully danced with the gods, and they've left a piece of their magic within you, a celestial keepsake. Ah, the beauty of a well-executed ritual—it's not a fleeting performance but an eternal imprint on your soul's journey. Now, how would you like to take a bow? Shall we explore what comes next in this mysterious and enchanting quest?

Effective Invocations, Prayers, and Mantras: The Lyrical Symphony of Sacred Words

The Craftsmanship Behind Every Word: Tailoring Your Invocations

If you've read my previous books, I put in a lot about crafting your desire, then I go over the usual ways to invoke a spirit. Invoking a spirit is only done after the intention is set and your statement of desire or intention written.

Now, imagine an artisan jeweler carefully selecting

gems to set in a ring. Each stone, with its unique luster and properties, contributes to the overall masterpiece. This is akin to choosing the words for your invocations. Each syllable carries a unique vibrational frequency, an innate power, and when woven together, creates a masterpiece that resonates through spiritual dimensions. These are not just words; they are the encoded keys to divine doors.

Picture this: you're standing in front of your altar, and the air is heavy with incense. You raise your arms and speak. Each word should be selected with the utmost care, not just for its surface meaning but its deeper esoteric significance. If invoking Aphrodite, the word "love" is more than an emotion; it's a cosmic force that moves heavens and mortal hearts alike. Mastery over your invocations is mastery over the sacred lexicon of the universe. When the right words are uttered in the right sequence, something extraordinary happens: the Universe leans in to listen.

The Melodic Curve: Rhythms, Cadence, and Intonation in Prayers

Think of a musician tuning their guitar before playing an important gig. The quality of sound isn't just about the skill of the musician, but also about the instrument being in perfect tune. Similarly, it's not just the words in your prayers, but the tone, the rhythm, and the cadence that count. This is the melody of your divine song, the vibrational wave that carries your intentions from your lips to the cosmic ears of the gods.

When you pray, don't just speak—sing. Whether through intonation or rhythmic repetition, the musical aspects of your prayers amplify their effectiveness. Perhaps you're chanting a mantra to Ganesh, the Elephant God, to remove obstacles in your life. The steady rhythm of the chant, in sync with your heartbeat, creates a harmony that reverberates through you and out into the cosmos. It's as if each beat is a knock on the divine door, growing louder and more insistent until, finally, it swings open.

Mantras: The Sacred Echo that Reverberates Through Eternity

Picture a pond, serene and still, with not a single ripple disturbing its surface. Now, imagine dropping a pebble into it; the impact creates a ripple that expands, reaches every shore, and echoes back to the center. Mantras work in a similar fashion. They are the pebble that disturbs the still waters of the Universe, and the effects ripple through reality, affecting change.

A mantra isn't a one-off utterance but a continuous echo in the grand cosmic auditorium. It doesn't fade; it accumulates power with repetition, like a chant that grows louder and more harmonious with each iteration. Your mantra is your spiritual signature, your cosmic ID, if you will, that resonates with the Universe. Picture your mantra as a sonic key, molded by your intent and honed by your focus. Once shaped, it's ready to unlock the treasure troves of cosmic gifts, from insight to blessings and beyond.

The incense has burned down, the candles flicker in their last moments, but the air is still thick with the presence of the divine. You've spoken, sung, and chanted. The Universe didn't just listen; it responded. Feel that tingling sensation on your skin? That's not mere static; that's the cosmic echo, a divine reply in a frequency that your soul understands.

Words are more than words. They are magical symbols, musical notes, and energetic frequencies, all wrapped into one. Just as a symphony can move us to tears and a well-written book can transport us to other worlds, so can your invocations, prayers, and mantras re-shape the very fabric of your reality. But what's that? You sense something more, a deeper layer beneath what you've just learned? Ah, my friend, you're right. Let's explore that, shall we?

The Significance of Offerings and Sacrifices: The Cosmic Love Language of Gifting

The Cosmic Exchange: Offerings as Spiritual Currency

The offerings. I also cover this in great detail with my other books. I'll take a bit different look in this book. Since I am in the film industry, I'll try to use analogies in the worlds of TV and movies.

You know the scene in the movie where the hero offers a valuable trinket to the guardian of a hidden temple? The offering is accepted, and the massive stone doors creak open, revealing treasures beyond imagination. That's not just Hollywood magic; that's an analogy for how offerings work in the spiritual world. Offerings are like the currency of the divine; you offer something of value to gain spiritual wealth or wisdom in return.

When you stand before your altar with an offering, be it incense, food, or something more symbolic, like a crafted talisman, you're not just placing an object; you're facilitating an exchange. Imagine you're at a cosmic market, and you're bargaining for divine favors or insights. The energies you're working with, whether gods, spirits, or universal forces, appreciate this cosmic currency. What you're essentially doing is making a bid at the auction of the arcane, and the spiritual forces can't resist but lean in, captivated by your offer.

The Weight of Sacrifice: Alchemy of Emotional and Material Investment

Remember, in epic fantasy shows when the lead characters have to make significant sacrifices to protect their kingdom or loved ones? The stakes are high, and the weight of the sacrifice adds gravity to the storyline. Similarly, the greater the sacrifice in your rituals, the more potent the rite becomes. A sacrifice isn't just an offering; it's an offering with emotional or material weight behind it.

Imagine you're about to perform a complex ritual that demands an object of personal significance—maybe a locket from a loved one or a handwritten journal. That item, imbued with emotional weight, becomes like the powerful, one-of-a-kind weapon in a fantasy tale. It's not just another blade; it's Excalibur. A sacrifice increases the magnetic pull of your ritual. Like the pivotal episode where heroes bring their ultimate weapon into play, your ritual too hits a climactic moment when sacrifices are made.

The Bond of Offering: Fostering Spiritual Relationships through Gifts

Think about your favorite romantic comedy. You know, the one where small gifts, accidental meet-ups, and awkward conversations gradually build up to a significant relationship? In much the same way, consistently offering gifts to the spirits or deities you work with fosters a growing relationship. An offering isn't just a onetime transaction; it's an installment in a long-term investment plan.

Imagine you've been working with Athena, the goddess of wisdom. You don't just offer olive oil once and ask for eternal wisdom. It's more like a friendship that you keep nurturing with gifts. Each offering is like sending a text message in a rom-com, keeping the conversation going. By sustaining this ritualistic 'chat,' you become familiar in the eyes of the divine. You move from being an occasional visitor to a recognized guest, invited to the deeper mysteries.

The air in your sacred space is filled with the tantalizing aroma of herbs, the gentle flicker of candlelight casting soft, golden glows on your face. You're no longer just a practitioner; you've become a cosmic philanthropist, a spiritual benefactor investing in divine stock. And oh, does it yield dividends! The incense may burn out, the food may be consumed, but what remains is an intangible yet very real bond with the sacred. Ah, the thrill of the gift, the mystery of the offer; it's far more than meets the eye, wouldn't you agree? On that tantalizing note, let's journey a little deeper, shall we?

Signs of a Successful Invocation: The Spiritual Echoes of Your Cosmic Call

A Symphony of Synchronicities: Real-world Reflections of Your Invocation

Recall the climactic episodes in fantasy TV shows where a character casts a powerful spell, and everything in the universe seems to respond—birds take flight, the wind howls, and arcane symbols glow. While your ritual space might not erupt in special effects, successful invocations echo in the fabric of your daily life through synchronicities.

You might find that after invoking Aphrodite, the goddess of love, you keep stumbling upon rose petals or heart shapes in unexpected places. Or perhaps, after calling upon Hermes for agility and wit, you notice an unusual number of references to winged sandals or messenger symbols in your life. Synchronicities are like the 'Easter eggs' in a well-crafted novel—a wink from the author, assuring you that your cosmic call has been heard and acknowledged.

Sometimes, these signs are so very subtle, you overlook them, so be on the lookout.

Emotional and Psychic Resonance: Feeling the Presence Beyond the Veil

Remember those scenes in books where the protagonist experiences a profound revelation, and there's this moment of emotional and psychic clarity? That sensation isn't confined to the pages of novels; it seeps into your ritual space too. The aftermath of a successful invocation often leaves you with an undeniable feeling of being 'touched' by something grander.

Suddenly, your intuition is sharper, akin to a detective in a mystery novel who starts putting the clues together. Or perhaps you feel an inexplicable rush of joy or peace, as if your emotional state has been fine-tuned by divine hands. You don't just 'think' something happened; you 'feel' it in every fiber of your being. Like the character who finds their purpose, you too stand in your circle, knowing something significant has unfolded.

Intriguing Mystical Phenomena: When the Invisible Becomes Almost Visible

Think about the moment in every suspenseful book or series when the unseen antagonist finally reveals a sliver of themselves—a shadow, a silhouette, a cryptic message. That's precisely what happens sometimes during or after a successful invocation: the mystical becomes almost tangible.

Perhaps the candle flames flicker in a pattern, or the incense smoke shapes itself like the sigil you drew. Maybe your divination tools provide shockingly accurate messages, echoing the essence of the entity you invoked. This isn't fiction; this is your ritual saying, "The call was successful; the line is connected." The deity or spirit is like an elusive character, offering a fleeting yet electrifying glimpse of their presence.

The room tingles with energy, and you find yourself glancing over your shoulder, almost expecting to see something—though you're not sure what. It's like reaching the end of a chapter where the storyline has twisted so enchantingly that you can't help but flip to the next page, eager for more revelations.

Before we go further, and begin our rituals to invoke Hermes and begin our voyage to the Akashic Records, a brief word about post-ritual grounding.

Grounding Post-Invocation: The Sacred Art of Cosmic Comeback

The Need for Energetic Rebalancing: A Cosmic Palette Cleanser

Back years ago, I was invited to be a judge in a barbecue cook-off, a contest to see who makes the best Texas Barbecue. In between samples of cooked beef or ribs, we'd take a sip of a beverage to cleanse our palette. This way, we're tasting the new sample with a fresh tongue. Grounding post-invocation is your energetic palette cleanser. When you've been mingling with cosmic energies, you've been sampling otherworldly flavors—rich, complex, and profoundly transformative. And while it's exhilarating to tap into this cosmic cuisine, you'll need to cleanse your energetic palate to fully savor your everyday experiences. Just like that sip of sparkling water, grounding is your body's way of re-establishing your internal balance.

Simple Grounding Techniques: A Spiritual Anchor

Imagine being a kite, your string stretching skyward, pulled by celestial winds. You've soared among the clouds, mingling with forces that regular kites can only dream of. But what happens to a kite that's never reeled back in? It risks getting lost, its fabric torn, and its frame damaged. Your grounding techniques are the hands that reel you back to Earth, offering stability and focus.

From deep belly-breathing to physically touching the ground, these are your spiritual anchors. They pull you back from your cosmic journey, yet they don't sever the connection; rather, they help you integrate these higher energies into your earthly existence. Think of grounding as the twist ending in a thriller novel—it reorients the entire narrative, making you revisit and appreciate everything you've been through.

Embrace the Mundane: Finding Beauty in the Everyday World

After grounding, the everyday world isn't just a place you return to; it's a realm re-enchanted by your magikal workings. Like the protagonist returning to their hometown at the end of a sweeping saga, you see your daily life through new lenses. A walk in the park becomes a stroll through a living altar, and the morning sunlight filtering through your window is nothing short of a divine blessing. Your grounding practices are not an end, but a beginning—a gateway to experiencing the extraordinary within the ordinary.

Alright, enough fooling around. Time to get after our journey to the mystical library - the Akashic Records! Man, I gotta speak to you about some important preparatory steps, like protection.

CHAPTER SIX

The Importance of Spiritual Protection: Your Cosmic Armor for Akashic Adventures

Guardian Forces: Your Spiritual Firewall

Let's kick off this conversation about spiritual protection with a familiar analogy: cybersecurity. We all know that browsing the internet without a proper firewall is like sailing into shark-infested waters without a cage. It's risky, to say the least. Now, diving into the Akashic Records is a lot like surfing the world wide web—full of infinite possibilities but not without its share of hazards. Just as a firewall filters unwanted data, guardian forces act as your spiritual firewall, providing an invisible yet impenetrable barrier between you and any entities or energies that mean harm.

Psychic Armor: The Fine Art of Energetic Bulletproofing

Picture a medieval knight before a jousting tournament. They don't just climb onto their horse and charge at full tilt; they armor up first. Your psychic armor is akin to this knight's steel plate—custom-fitted, lightweight but robust. Learning how to suit up energetically not only shields you but also elevates your confidence. It's like going on stage in a stunning outfit—you feel invincible, ready to take on the world, or in this case, other realms.

The Layered Shielding: A Symphony of Protective Measures

Now, consider an onion's structure—multiple layers, each serving as a line of defense. A single layer might be penetrable, but together they create a sturdy, almost impenetrable mass. In the same way, your spiritual protection isn't just a one-and-done operation. It's a combination—a symphony of multiple energetic techniques, shields, and rituals. From invoking protective deities to constructing energetic bubbles, each layer you add enriches the protective melody surrounding you, making it more and more resilient.

With your spiritual firewall activated, your psychic armor lustrously shining, and your layered shields humming their protective symphony, you become an unassailable fortress. But don't forget—fortresses are not just built to keep things out; they're also designed to safely let the right things in. Like an expert DJ mixing tracks, your protective measures allow you to harmonize with the Akashic Records, drawing out the sweetest, most transformative tunes while leaving the noise behind. So go ahead, flip to the next page!

Crafting and Using Magikal Shields: Your Personal Forcefield in the Akashic Journey

The Alchemy of Shield Creation: Mixing Ingredients with Intent

You know those cooking shows where chefs carefully pick each ingredient, considering its flavor, texture, and how it complements the other components of the dish? Crafting a magikal shield is pretty much the culinary art of the metaphysical world. Every element, from the intention you set to the sigils you might use, acts as an ingredient in this mystical recipe. And just like in cooking, the fresher and purer your ingredients, the more effective and potent the end result.

The Mechanics of Energetic Architecture: Building the Shield

When constructing a skyscraper, architects take into account load-bearing walls, wind resistance, and a host of other variables. Crafting your shield is similar—it's your personal skyscraper in the etheric realm. Once you've chosen your "ingredients," you'll need to assemble them through visualization, meditation, and, of course, magikal energy flow. It's not just about stacking bricks; it's about understanding the interplay between each brick, the mortar that holds them, and the elements they'll be exposed to. Visualize the intricate lattice of your shield, almost like spider silk but as robust as steel, each strand imbued with your intent and willpower.

Activation and Maintenance: The Power Switch and Upkeep

Even the most sophisticated computer system needs regular updates and a good old restart now and then. Your magikal shield is no exception. After all, you wouldn't wear the same set of clothes indefinitely without washing them, right? Keeping your shield 'clean' and 'charged' requires a form of spiritual upkeep. Activating it isn't like flicking a light switch; it's more like turning a dial. The more you fine-tune this dial, the better your shield becomes at discerning what to keep out and what to let through.

In an Akashic expedition, consider your magikal shield as your all-terrain vehicle, customized and tailored just for you. Not only does it protect, but it also enhances the journey, making the uncharted terrains of the Akashic Records less intimidating and more insightful. As you become comfortable with your shield, it will almost seem like an extension of you, a second skin that's not merely defensive but also empowers you to interact with these spiritual landscapes in more meaningful ways.

So are you ready to turn the page? You're about to learn how this shield synchronizes with other navigational tools you'll need for your Akashic adventure. Keep reading; your spiritual toolkit is about to get a remarkable upgrade.

Employing Guardian Spirits: Your Spiritual A-Team for Akashic Exploration

Identifying Your Guardian Spirits: Auditions for Your Celestial Cast

Picture this: You're the director of a blockbuster film. Who you cast in the lead roles can make or break the entire project. In the Akashic realm, your guardian spirits are your A-listers. It's crucial to know how to discern between a genuine spirit guide and a cosmic extra looking for a feature role in your spiritual journey. Intuition and intention are your casting directors, giving you the inner 'gut feeling' that assures you of your spirit guides' authenticity.

Establishing a Connection: The Script and Dialog

Think of communicating with your guardian spirits as working with seasoned actors; they know their lines but also value an improv moment. For your dialog to flow naturally, you'll need a script—a pre-determined set of intentions and questions to guide your interactions. Yet, remain open to unexpected, profound wisdom that comes unscripted. Imagine you're in a rehearsal, and the actor suddenly goes off-script, delivering a line so powerful it brings everyone to tears. That's the kind of unexpected insight a genuine connection with your guardian spirit can offer.

Setting Boundaries: The Director's Cut

Even the most dedicated actors have boundaries—no dangerous stunts or overstepping personal lines. The same goes for your guardian spirits. Setting boundaries isn't about constraining; it's about directing the energy effectively. Make it clear what you're willing to explore and what remains off-limits. It's like stating that your movie won't have any high-risk action scenes; it sets the stage for a certain kind of narrative, one where all parties feel respected and engaged.

With your celestial A-team by your side, traversing the Akashic Records becomes less of a solo expedition and more of an ensemble cast adventure. Each spirit guide brings their unique 'talents' to the table, enriching your spiritual screenplay.

So what comes next, you ask? As we say in the film business… Check the gate! Moving on to the next setup!

Talismans and Gemstones for Protection: Your Alchemical

Shield and Astral Key

The Metaphysical Essence: Your Own Astral Palette

Imagine you are a spellcaster standing before an alchemist's bench, populated with curious flasks, swirling potions, and arcane glyphs. Now, among these mystical ingredients are gemstones and talismans, each whispering in ethereal tongues about their power and potential. Picture an amethyst as a vial of astral tranquility or a tiger's eye as a rune of grounding force. Selecting the right gem or talisman is like choosing the perfect ingredient for a spell. You need to grasp the metaphysical essences of these materials, the "color palette" for your astral artwork, so to speak. Each choice opens or closes doors in the unseen world, so choose wisely.

The Ritual of Bonding: Your Spell of Affinity

After selecting the right gem or talisman, you can't just hang it around your neck and gallivant into the Akashic Records. That would be like casting a spell without the proper incantation. It needs to be attuned to your energy through a ritual of bonding. Picture this ritual as etching your name into an enchanted scroll that forms a magical contract between you and your chosen object. This isn't a casual affair; it's an intimate dance of energies that cements your alliance with the talisman. Just like you wouldn't hastily scribble in a book of shadows, you won't want to skimp on this ritual.

Combining Shields: The Magical Symphony

Perhaps you've been considering the idea that one talisman might not be enough. You're correct; it's not unlike having multiple layers of magical shielding. Imagine wielding not just a wand but also a staff and a dagger, each enchanted with different protective spells. When combined, they create a harmonious magical symphony, a protective aura of unparalleled complexity and power. An obsidian pendant for warding off negative energies might sing in harmony with a selenite bracelet for spiritual clarity. When curated thoughtfully, they become a cosmic orchestra, protecting you from a myriad of unseen influences.

Spiritual Maintenance: The Potion of Renewal

Yes, even the arcane needs maintenance. If you've noticed a diminishing glow or a subtle depletion in energy, it might be time to refresh your talismans and gemstones. Imagine each one like a potion bottle; over time, the liquid evaporates and loses its potency. Recharging them is like adding fresh ingredients and giving the potion a good stir. A moonlight bath for your moonstone or a sage cleansing for your quartz—each gem and talisman has its preferred method of energetic renewal. Never let your magical arsenal collect astral dust!

Recognizing the Cycle: The Season of Your Magic

Lastly, understand that everything in magik has a lifecycle. Even spells wane and potions expire. Your talismans and gemstones are no different. As a responsible spellcaster, recognize the signs of an ending cycle. It might be a change in color, a breakage, or simply a felt change in energy. These are not signs of failure, but of evolution. It may be time to respectfully retire that item, and in its place, discover something new that resonates with your current spiritual state.

With these intricate facets of wisdom in hand, you are ready to not just survive but thrive within the mystical archives of the Akashic Records. But oh, don't relax just yet. Our next layer of understanding awaits, not just to unveil the world around you, but also to unlock the mysteries within. Ah, the allure of internal alchemy calls, doesn't it?

Purification Rituals: The Gatekeepers of Your Akashic Journey

Understanding the Essence of Purification

Think of a ritual of purification as the magical swipe of a keycard granting you access to a restricted library. In this case, it's the Akashic Records—an expanse so sacred, so spiritually ripe that it demands your utmost purity. Purification isn't merely the absence of negativity; it's a cultivation of balanced, harmonious energy. Like tuning a musical instrument before a grand symphony, this ensures that your vibrational frequency is compatible with the Akashic frequencies. Your journey to and from these celestial archives will benefit enormously if you step forth in purity.

Selection of Elements: The Building Blocks of Your Ritual

Envision your ritual as a handcrafted potion, a blend of carefully chosen magical elements. Each element—be it water, fire, air, or earth—has a unique vibrational quality, akin to different ingredients in a spell. The process of selection is the first step toward creating a balanced, efficient ritual. As you sift through your magical toolbox, consider herbs like sage or rosemary, or gemstones like clear quartz or selenite, always focusing on their individual magical attributes. Carefully marrying these elements can yield a far more potent and effective ritual.

Sequence and Timing: The Symphony of Actions

An effective ritual is not a jumbled cacophony of actions, but a fluid sequence, like musical notes arranged in a specific order. Each part of the ritual holds significance, as does the order in which they are performed. Do you cast a circle before lighting the incense, or the other way around? What about the timing of your verbal incantations? These are not random; they're choreographed steps in your spiritual dance. The cadence and tempo of your actions can be the difference between a clumsy entry and an elegant passage into the Akashic domain.

The Duality of Purification: Pre and Post-Access

Imagine boarding a ship to a new land. Just as you wouldn't bring invasive species to a pristine ecosystem, you'd also not want to bring something harmful back home. That's why your ritual of purification is twofold. Pre-access rituals cleanse your energetic aura, providing you with the necessary clearance to enter this high-vibrational space. Post-access rituals act like a magical decontamination chamber, safeguarding your own spiritual ecosystem from any unwanted energies you might have encountered. Both are vital chapters in the story of your Akashic journey.

Mindfulness and Intention: The Subtle Spices of Your Ritual

In a recipe, the difference between a dish and a masterpiece often lies in the subtle spices. In my case, the difference between MY barbecue and what you'd find in a restaurant is the spice mix I use. The same holds true for rituals. The subtleties are your mindfulness and intention. Imagine them as the magical glue binding the elements of your ritual. Each movement, each word, each breath should be saturated with your focused intention. This is not the time for mental drifting; your consciousness must be as sharp as a ceremonial blade. The quality of your mindfulness directly influences the potency of your ritual. Simply put, be present or risk a diluted experience.

And so, armed with the wisdom of purification rituals, you're not just a visitor to the Akashic Records—you're an honored guest. It's like having a VIP backstage pass to the mysteries of the universe. But oh, we've barely scratched the surface! Coming up next are additional layers of expertise that will turn you into the ultimate spiritual archivist. How tantalizing to think that, with each page turned, the secrets of your existence become less opaque, more accessible. What a spellbinding journey it is, wouldn't you agree?

CHAPTER SEVEN

Visualization Practices: Your Inner Lens to the Akashic Records

The Foundation of Inner Imagery

Imagine this: You have a magical telescope, intricately carved with ancient runes. Through its lens, you're able to peek into other dimensions and untangle the mysteries of the universe. Well, guess what? You already possess such a tool. It's not made of brass or glass, but of thought and consciousness. This is your ability to visualize. Just like you can't point a telescope anywhere and expect to see wonders, you need to know how to focus your internal lens.

Developing Crystal-Clear Focus

You see, the potency of your visualization journey begins with how well you can create and sustain a clear mental image. Think of it like tuning a magical instrument—too fuzzy, and the melody is lost; too rigid, and the harmony snaps. Therefore, mastering focus is like finding the right note that resonates with the Akashic field. To do this, you'll need to practice short sessions where you maintain a single mental image for a few minutes at a time. Just like an athlete exercises to build muscle, you must train your mind to hold a vivid image in your inner eye.

The Role of Emotion and Senses

But it's not just about seeing. True visualization is an immersive experience. How would you feel walking through a forest of wisdom, where each tree is a living book in the Akashic Library? Can you hear the leaves whispering arcane knowledge, feel the texture of the sacred ground beneath your feet? The more senses you involve, the more lifelike your visualization becomes. Think of it as adding spices to a potion; each sense enlivens the magical brew that is your visualization.

The Importance of Anchoring Symbols

In visualization, symbols act like signposts guiding you through a mystical landscape. They serve as anchors, a sort of magical shorthand that captures a complex idea or energy in an easily recognizable form. A staircase leading up might signify ascending to higher knowledge, while a key could symbolize unlocking hidden wisdom. These aren't merely decorations on your mental scenery; they are integral aspects of the journey. Attach personal meaning to these symbols, and they become like familiar friends accompanying you on your spiritual adventures.

Adaptive Techniques for Advanced Practitioners

As you deepen your practice, you'll discover that your initial techniques, though useful, might not cover the breadth of experiences awaiting you. There are multiple levels of Akashic access, each with its unique challenges and wonders. Imagine a painter who starts with only primary colors and then learns the art of mixing shades. Gradually you'll incorporate advanced techniques like layering multiple visualizations or even shifting perspectives within a single visualization. Each adds a new layer of depth, a new nuance to your Akashic exploration.

With these key principles at your disposal, you're ready to sharpen that internal telescope and venture far beyond the ordinary limits of knowledge and reality. But wait—before you're lost in awe at the vastness of the Akashic Records, remember that like any seasoned traveler, you'll need a reliable map. Coming up, we'll discuss just that—the invaluable guidelines and ethics you must heed while journeying in such an exalted space. Trust me, these aren't trivial add-ons; they're the bread and butter of any ethical Akashic explorer. What awaits you are keys to doors you never knew existed.

Meditative Pathways: The Stairways to the Center of Reality

Let me share an episode that forever changed my understanding of the Akashic Records and the power of meditative pathways. Imagine a colossal staircase, each step fashioned from gleaming, iridescent stone. Each ascension was like walking on a different plane of reality. This wasn't a quick jaunt; it felt like a monumental expedition into the heart of existence. Ascending, it felt like each stairway was a chapter, a layer peeled back to reveal another tantalizing glimpse into a grand design. This, my friends, is the might of meditation. It's not just a simple relaxation technique; it's a chariot that can transport you into the crux of reality itself.

It's the technique I use in my High Self Meditation I sell online. Check the "About" page in the back.

Basic Mindfulness: Your Starting Point

To set foot on these grand stairways, you must first clear the path. Basic mindfulness acts as a broom, sweeping away the mundane thoughts cluttering your mind. But this is no ordinary sweeping; think of it as tidying up your inner sanctuary. You make room for the sacred, for the incredible, for the ineffable. As you sit in a comfortable posture, close your eyes and draw your attention to your breath. In and out, slow and steady, until you feel a sense of inner stillness envelop you.

Breath as a Vehicle: Propelling Forward

Your breath isn't just air; it's your vehicle, your chariot of fire. It carries you forward, upward. You've got to fuel it right to make it glide smoothly. Breathing techniques, like diaphragmatic breathing or the 4-7-8 method, aren't just physical acts. They are rituals that consecrate your meditative journey. Focus on your breath as if it's a ritual incantation, a sacred phrase that holds the promise of enlightenment.

Releasing Distractions: The Price of Admission

On your journey, you'll encounter doors, gates, and checkpoints. To pass through, you'll need to pay a price, and the currency is your attachments. Releasing distractions is like paying the toll on a mystical highway. Every thought about what's for dinner or what someone said is like a toll booth slowing you down. Acknowledge these thoughts, and then let them go. This is your ticket to proceed unburdened.

Visualization Alongside Meditation: Adding Vivid Colors

Remember that stairway I told you about? Now it's your turn to build it in your mind. But this isn't just architectural work; it's an act of spiritual sculpting. You craft each stair, each landing, each door you pass through, using your mind's palette. Here, your visualization skills come in handy. Visualize each step as a sacred rune, glowing softly, guiding you higher and higher. The more vividly you can imagine this ascent, the more real the journey becomes.

Affirmations: Your Guiding Verses

As you ascend each step, what do you hear? Are there guiding verses, magical affirmations that embolden you to continue? Yes! Think of affirmations as your personal spells that instill you with courage and intent. When you're halfway up those ethereal steps and fatigue starts to creep in, reciting an affirmation like "I am attuned to the wisdom of the Universe" can be the wind beneath your wings.

The Summit: Transcendent Integration

And then, you reach the summit, a point so pure, so elevated, it defies description. This is where your soul commingles with the Akashic fabric, where questions dissolve into understanding. You're not just a visitor; you're a participant in a cosmic dialogue. It's akin to suddenly realizing you've been a part of a masterpiece painting while viewing it.

At the summit, take your time. Relish the aura of enlightenment, the newfound wisdom, and the ineffable beauty surrounding you. When you're ready, make your descent. But remember, you're not just coming back; you're bringing something with you—a fragment of eternal wisdom, a keepsake from the very core of reality.

The stairway isn't going anywhere. It waits for you, a permanent structure in your spiritual landscape, becoming richer, more intricate with each sojourn. It's here every time you want it, or need it. As for what comes next, let's just say there are realms and pathways that defy human language, awaiting your courageous footsteps. So, lace up those metaphysical boots, my friends. A grand adventure beckons, and the stairway you've built is just the beginning.

Scrying: The Mystical Art of Seeing Beyond
Personal Struggles: My Dance with Scrying

When I first began to explore scrying, I'll admit it was like trying to find a black cat in a dark room using a short match. Well, maybe it's more like an old, predigital radio. There's a lot of static before you can lock onto a clear frequency. Hours, days, and what felt like years passed with me staring into a bowl of water (my daughter's favorite method), a crystal ball, or even into the depths of a flickering candle flame. I kept waiting for that "a-ha" moment, the time when the mists would part and wisdom would flow. My patience was running out, but something in me insisted on persevering. Finally, one fateful evening, the ripples in the water gave way to symbols, a clear vision. It was as if the Universe had decided I had earned my seat at the cosmic theater.

When accessing the Akashic Records, scrying will assist you in mapping the pathways. So, allow me a slight detour here for a bit.

Elemental Choice: Picking Your Scrying Medium

Embarking on the scrying journey first requires you to choose your vessel, your elemental medium. Water, fire, air, earth — each offers a different cinematic experience, so to speak. Imagine you're in a grand library, but instead of books, the shelves are lined with different elements. Your choice of element sets the stage for the type of visions you'll receive. A crystal ball is like a wide-screen IMAX theater, perfect for larger-than-life revelations, while a bowl of water offers a more intimate, nuanced narrative.

Setting the Atmosphere: Sanctifying Your Space

Before you get lost in the depths of your chosen

medium, pay attention to the surrounding space. This isn't just about lighting some candles and dimming the lights; it's about creating a sanctuary. Consider the scents in the air, the fabric beneath you, even the cup of tea by your side. These elements don't just enhance your focus; they're the supporting cast in your mystical drama, bringing depth and dimension to your quest.

Stilling the Mind: The Scrying Mantra

As you settle in, it's tempting to rush the moment, to aggressively seek the vision. But you can't force a flower to bloom, and you can't pressure the cosmic consciousness to reveal itself. Instead, center your thoughts, perhaps even adopt a scrying mantra. This mantra is like a backstage pass, granting you exclusive access to this mystical performance. The mantra I personally used during my struggling phase was "Vision flows, wisdom knows." It was a gentle reminder to relinquish control and allow the vision to come to me.

Interpretation: The Subtlety and Complexity

When the visions finally come, it's like a breakthrough in a detective story, that instant when a seemingly random collection of clues suddenly makes sense. But hold your horses; interpretation is a layered affair. Sometimes what you see could be symbolic rather than literal. For instance, a vision of a falling tower may not indicate an actual disaster, but could symbolize a drastic change or upheaval in life. The key to accurate interpretation is to keep an open, yet discerning mind. Think of yourself as an archeologist, delicately dusting off each revelation to uncover its true meaning.

So, there you have it. Scrying isn't a sprint; it's a marathon, a deeply rewarding lifelong pursuit. Even when it seems like you're stuck in a cosmic traffic jam, the beauty of the journey itself is worth more than words can express. When you finally break through, the vistas you will see are beyond magnificent. They're not just messages; they're poetry written by the universe, intimate letters from the cosmic to the individual, giving a taste of the grandeur that lies beyond our everyday perception.

Feel the call? Remember, the medium is waiting, and the universe is always ready to send its next message. Your task is to prepare yourself to be the best receiver you can be. It's an ongoing adventure, an ever-unfolding tapestry of insight and illumination. And the journey is just as crucial as the destination. With the right mindset, perseverance, and a touch of cosmic luck, you too will see beyond the here and now. Keep looking, keep asking, keep scrying, and the universe will respond in whispers, visions, and flashes of awe-inspiring clarity.

Utilizing Astral Projection: Your Celestial Passport to the Akashic Records

The Seed of Intention: Why Astral Projection?

There's an old saying that the journey of a thousand miles begins with a single step. When it comes to navigating the realms of the Akashic Records, that step begins not with your feet but with your very essence—your astral self. Think of your physical body as your home, filled with comfort and familiarity. Astral projection is akin to stepping out of that cozy sanctuary and exploring the cosmos. It's like your very own space expedition, where instead of rockets and space suits, you're using your astral self to traverse dimensions.

I prefer astral travel to access the Records, often meeting up a guide or Hermes. For me, it's a bit easier and I use a private version of my high self-meditation, which takes me to the center of creation, then anywhere else I wish to travel. It's all just a thought away!

Astral Prep School: The Importance of Mental Readiness

Before astronauts jet off into space, they undergo extensive training. In the same vein, astral projection requires a foundational level of mental preparation. You're not just taking a walk in the park; you're journeying into spaces that are as magnificent as they are overwhelming. A distracted or agitated mind is like traveling with a foggy windshield—you'll miss the sights and could even veer off course. So sharpen your mental focus. Techniques like mindfulness and basic meditation aren't just good skills; they're prerequisites. Consider them your astral SATs, and you've got to score high to gain entry into the celestial university that is the Akashic Records.

Navigational Strategies: Guiding the Astral Self

Would you ever set sail on uncharted waters without a compass or a map? Of course not! Similarly, astral projection calls for some form of direction. You can visualize this as weaving a silver cord from your physical body to your astral form, a shimmering thread of energy that will guide you back to the earthly plane when your journey is complete. You could also think of a specific symbol or phrase that acts as your North Star, a focal point to guide you through the astral wilderness. These navigational cues are not only your roadmap but also your safety net. They ensure you roam without losing yourself in the majestic expanse.

Field Notes and Recollections: Documenting Your Experience

As you start to navigate the astral realms, think of

yourself as an explorer, charting new territories. What you see, hear, or even feel is data, precious information that needs to be recorded. Because, believe me, the awe and wonder can make memories fuzzy. Once you're back in your physical body, jot down your experiences. They're more than just fascinating anecdotes; they're firsthand accounts of otherworldly realms. Imagine that you're compiling an astral travelogue, one that not only enriches your understanding but might help others someday when they embark on similar quests.

Reentry Protocol: Safely Returning to Your Physical Shell

Your astral odyssey may feel like an endless cascade of wonder, but remember, you have a home to return to—your physical body. Reentry is just as crucial as departure. Visualize your astral self slowly merging back into your physical form, like a droplet of water rejoining the ocean. This isn't just a matter of snapping back; it's a gentle merging, a thoughtful reunification of the celestial and terrestrial aspects of you. Once you're back, take some time to adjust. Imagine you've just returned from a world tour; you need a moment to let it all sink in, to truly appreciate the grandiosity of the journey you just undertook.

There we are! Astral projection isn't something to be rushed or taken lightly. It's a commitment, an undertaking that needs time, energy, and heaps of respect. You are, after all, stepping into the most sacred libraries of existence. But oh, the rewards! Imagine gazing upon the sum total of all human experiences, witnessing the birth of stars, understanding the threads that weave the very fabric of reality. I won't say it's easy, but by the cosmic forces, it's worthwhile.

So here you stand, on the precipice of unimaginable discovery. The Akashic Records await you, a labyrinth of cosmic wisdom that your astral self is now equipped to explore. You've got your celestial passport, your navigational cues, and a heart full of courage. It's time for your grand odyssey into the Akashic wonders, and the only question now is, are you ready to fly?

Confirming Successful Entry into the Records: How to Know You're Not Just Dreaming

Landing Marks: Recognizing Akashic Signatures

So you've projected your astral form, navigated through celestial pathways, and arrived... somewhere. But how do you know you've actually reached the Akashic Records? Picture this—you've navigated a maze, and at its heart lies an enchanted garden. But any garden has its unique flora, right? Similarly, the Akashic Records have their own unmistakable signatures—vibrations, colors, even sounds—that set them apart from other astral locations. Just as a botanist recognizes a rare orchid by its unique pattern, you'll start to notice specific energetic imprints that signal your arrival in this celestial repository. These signatures are your first confirmation, your tactile 'hello' from the Records.

Emotional Resonance: The Gut Feeling of Being in the Right Place

Imagine going home after a long journey. The moment you step through the door, you're washed over by a feeling of familiarity and warmth, as if the walls themselves welcome you. This intuitive sense of 'rightness'—a deep emotional resonance—parallels what you'll experience upon entering the Akashic Records. That gut feeling isn't just nostalgia or sentiment; it's your very soul acknowledging the sacredness of the space you've entered. Don't underestimate the power of intuition here. Just as a homecoming can bring a tear to your eye, this emotional resonance is a genuine, palpable acknowledgment that you've arrived.

Interactive Checkpoints: Asking Questions and Receiving Answers

Do you recall those choose-your-own-adventure books where your decisions dictated the storyline? Navigating the Akashic Records involves a similar dynamic interaction. You can 'ask'—through thought, emotion, or astral intent—whether you've reached the Records. Expect responsive confirmations, not in the form of a nodding librarian but through signs, symbols, or even emotions that effectively answer your query. It's akin to asking a tree in the enchanted forest if you're going the right way, and seeing a branch subtly point you forward. This interaction sets the Akashic Records apart from just any astral plane. It's a responsive environment, one that communicates if you know how to ask and listen.

Subtle, Yet Profound Shifts in Perception: Seeing Through New Lenses

Remember your first pair of prescription glasses? The world snapped into focus in a way you didn't even know was possible. Entering the Akashic Records instigates a similar perceptual shift, where the astral fog lifts and the spiritual topography becomes crystal clear. You may even start perceiving information as holographic texts, interconnected webs, or cascading waterfalls of symbols. These aren't your everyday astral sights. The Records have a transcendent clarity that reframes your spiritual vision, another confirmation that you've graduated from the ordinary astral dimensions into a realm of higher wisdom.

The Internal Oracle: Your Inner Knowing Affirms Your Location

At last, there's an intrinsic, unshakeable knowing that you've arrived—an inner oracle that rings its celestial bell inside your soul. This isn't something that can be easily described but is felt profoundly. It's as if every fiber of your being hums in unison, singing a cosmic tune that resonates with the frequencies of the Records. This isn't just any tune but a symphony of enlightenment, a musical affirmation that you're exactly where you need to be, enveloped by universal wisdom.

Now that you've crossed the astral threshold and you've felt the vivid confirmations, both emotional and interactive, you'll notice something else. It's a certain quality in the astral air, a weightiness filled with purpose and silent anticipation, like the moments before the curtain lifts on a grand stage play. What role will you play in this drama of cosmic exploration? What wisdom will you unearth from these celestial vaults?

So breathe, absorb, and prepare to fully immerse yourself in the Akashic Records. This isn't merely a chapter of your astral journey but a whole volume of enlightenment, and your soul is the ink, writing its story in the celestial codex. Your spiritual expedition has led you here, and it's more than an astral pit stop; it's a spiritual homecoming. What unfolds next is not just page-turning—it's soul-stirring.

CHAPTER EIGHT

Recognizing Akashic Landmarks: Navigating the Ever-Changing Landscape

The Fluidity of the Akashic Landscape

Let's play with a mental scenario. Imagine you're stepping into a living art gallery where each painting morphs and dances before your eyes. One moment, you see landscapes; the next, swirling galaxies. There's a reason this cosmic tapestry doesn't hold still—it's alive! Just as Earth's landscapes change with the seasons, the Akashic Records are no fixed destination but an evolving realm that mirrors the dynamism of collective consciousness. Don't expect the celestial hills and astral streams you saw last time to remain in place. They might have transformed into crystalline cliffs or luminous lakes. The realm dances to the rhythm of universal energy flows, and each visit offers a fresh landscape for you to navigate.

Personalized Landscapes: Your Soul's Unique Scenery

Picture yourself at a masquerade ball, each guest wearing a mask uniquely crafted to match their personality. In much the same way, the Akashic Records interact with each visitor, molding themselves into landscapes that resonate with individual spiritual vibrations. You and your best friend could visit at the same time, and yet your experiences could be as different as a snowflake and a desert rose. This is because the Akashic realm not only stores information but also interprets your energetic signature, presenting itself in ways that will most resonate with your current state of being.

Anchors in a Shifting Terrain: Consistent Markers

As changeable as the Akashic terrain might be, think of it as a forest with both wandering paths and solid landmarks. You may not encounter the same celestial waterfall twice, but certain elements serve as universal touchstones. These could be massive pillars of light, vortexes of energy, or even unique color palettes that signify specific types of information. They're akin to North Stars in the astral sky, guiding you through your exploration. These markers are your "home base," a place to return to if you find yourself disoriented in this constantly shifting environment.

Time-Space Variations: A Journey in Non-Linear Dimensions

Do you remember the first time you tasted something spicy? Time slowed, senses heightened, and suddenly, your attention focused entirely on that singular moment. Now, think of the Akashic Records as existing in a non-linear time-space fabric. While earthly landmarks like Stonehenge or the pyramids remain in place across centuries, Akashic landmarks operate outside our concept of linear time. It means you could witness the origins of a star in one moment and glimpse a far-off future civilization in the next. Recognizing these time-space landmarks is key to successful navigation. It adds layers to your understanding, helping you connect seemingly unrelated dots into a cosmic narrative.

So, you see, your relationship with the Akashic Records is a dynamic dance of recognition and discovery. With each visit, you refine your understanding, as the scenery itself morphs to reveal new facets of cosmic wisdom. And just when you think you have the terrain all mapped out, it surprises you with new aspects, new markers, and new lessons. It's like having a series of enlightening conversations with a wise elder who knows just when to change the topic to keep you intrigued.

You learn to find familiarity amid the unfamiliar,

comfort in the evolving, and you start to recognize the landmarks not just as external checkpoints but as reflections of your own soul's journey. You get comfortable with change because you realize that constancy isn't the point; the point is the experience itself—the quest for wisdom that each unique, ever-changing landscape offers you.

And speaking of quests, have you ever wondered about the inhabitants of this celestial landscape? We've talked about recognizing the terrain, but what about its spiritual denizens? Well, just like any landscape on Earth has its wildlife, so too does the Akashic terrain. But here, the wildlife is not of flesh and feathers but of wisdom and archetypes.

The promise of meeting these celestial entities, of interacting with archetypal wisdom, is as thrilling as the landscape itself. As we glide further into the heart of the Akashic, you will learn how to communicate with these entities, gather knowledge from them, and even create partnerships for your spiritual advancement.

But that's a conversation for another moment, a moment as unique and captivating as the Akashic landscape itself. For now, breathe in the astral air, look around, and remember: you're not just a visitor but a vital part of this ever-changing, ever-inspiring celestial tapestry.

Engaging with Akashic Entities: The Unseen Librarians of the Cosmic Library

The Who's Who of the Akashic Landscape

Imagine walking into the Library of Congress, but instead of librarians bustling about in their everyday attire, you see enigmatic beings of light, scholars in astral form, and historians from dimensions you never knew existed. The Akashic Records are teeming with life forms that defy earthly categorization. Let's meet the main players, shall we? There are spirits whose sole duty is to maintain the Records, akin to curators of a grand museum. Then there are historians, researchers, and other astral entities that sift through the pages of cosmic chronicles, piecing together intricate tapestries of interstellar narratives.

The Art of Approach: Etiquette in the Akashic Halls

Just as you wouldn't burst into a professor's office without knocking, there are codes of conduct when engaging with these Akashic entities. They don't deal in mortal currency; what they value is intention and respect. Be mentally prepared with well-defined queries or areas of exploration. Imagine having a cosmic key, your intention, that fits perfectly into a celestial lock, opening doors to rooms filled with the specific wisdom you seek. But be cautious; this key should be crafted with the purest metals of sincerity and respect.

Dynamic Interactions: Conversations with Cosmic Librarians

You might think of engaging with these entities as some sort of formal, ritualistic exchange. But let's shatter that stereotype. It's more like having tea with a wise elder. They don't expect you to come prepared with a list of formal questions, scripted and rehearsed. Instead, they welcome a flow of thought, where one idea cascades into another. If Earthly librarians assist you in finding books or resources, these Akashic librarians guide you to energetic imprints and thought forms, the building blocks of the Records themselves.

Tips for Successful Dialog: Keep an Astral Notebook

Having a notebook while navigating earthly libraries is considered smart, but having an "astral notebook" while cruising the Akashic Records is nothing short of genius. Yes, it's a metaphorical notebook, where you jot down your inner thoughts, your questions, and the flashes of insight you gain during these interactions. You don't need pen and paper; your mind will do the scribbling. This astral notebook serves as your memoir, capturing the moments, thoughts, and wisdom that you will want to revisit and decode once you're back in your terrestrial form.

Let me share a secret. The first time I tried to engage with these astral entities, it felt like I was fumbling in a cosmic party where I knew no one. I carried with me an awkward blend of curiosity and hesitation. The Akashic entities, sensing my genuine desire to learn but also my hesitations, played it cool. I remember how one spirit, radiant like a sun yet comforting as moonlight, guided me to a particular corner of the Records where I found wisdom specifically attuned to my queries. It was as if the Records themselves whispered, "You're not alone. We're here to guide you."

The experience taught me it's not about what you ask; it's about the energy behind the asking. The way I see it, these entities are not gatekeepers, but facilitators, helping you unlock the doors you didn't even know existed.

Learning to converse with them is like learning a new language, a language not of words but of energies and intentions. The more fluent you become, the deeper you can explore, and the more spectacular your findings. You're like a cosmic archaeologist, sifting through layers of universal wisdom, and these entities are your guides, showing you where to dig.

And this is the moment where we pivot, ever so slightly, like a dancer making a graceful turn. We've laid the groundwork on how to engage with the Akashic entities. But what happens when you want to go beyond engagement to forge meaningful partnerships with these beings for spiritual growth? Ah, that's when the adventure intensifies, a step into an even grander arena of possibilities. Are you prepared to explore alliances with these cosmic entities, these guardians of interdimensional wisdom? If the idea tickles your curiosity, I assure you, dear reader, the next revelation will stir your very soul.

The Akashic Records

So, you've arrived. You've navigated the intricacies of astral travel and perhaps met some of the cosmic librarians who roam these hallowed corridors. But now comes the real reason you ventured into the Akashic Records: to glean insight, retrieve knowledge, and decode information. Friends, it's not an understatement to say that this is where the magic happens. Or should I say, this is where your soul recognizes its essence through the wisdom stored here.

Recognizing the Formats of Information

To start, you must understand that the Akashic Records are not confined to pages of a book or scrolls in a cabinet. The wisdom you seek may manifest as intricate patterns, like mandalas woven by the hand of the universe itself. On one occasion, I found myself interpreting an elaborate dance performance by ethereal beings. In another instance, the insight

I sought flowed through a haunting melody that I later translated into words. So, the first step is becoming open to multiple modes of understanding—visual, auditory, and even emotional.

The Role of Intuition

Intuition is your best friend here. If you've ever played a musical instrument by ear, you know how melodies can be plucked from the air, without sight-reading a single note. In a similar vein, intuition allows you to "tune in" to the frequencies of the Akashic Records. Don't be surprised if you're drawn to a specific tome or section without apparent reason. Your soul is like a divining rod, pointing you towards the wisdom you seek.

Ask Specific Questions

Asking the right questions is akin to entering the right search query into Google. If you're too vague, you'll get a plethora of unrelated information. Ask specific questions, as it will narrow down your search and yield more accurate answers. Imagine you're a cosmic detective, piecing together a celestial puzzle. Being precise in your queries can be the difference between finding a missing piece or adding clutter to your investigation.

Be Prepared for Symbolic Language

Picture yourself decoding ancient hieroglyphs without a Rosetta stone. Sounds daunting, right? But consider that your intuition is that Rosetta stone. In the Akashic Records, truth often comes veiled in metaphors and symbols. Yet, when deciphered, these symbols reveal layers of nuanced wisdom. I recall a moment when I viewed a client's tapestry made entirely of golden thread. At first, it seemed abstract, but as I looked closer, I realized each twist and knot conveyed a hidden message.

Managing Information Overload

Given that you are tapping into cosmic wisdom, it's easy to be overwhelmed. Imagine wandering into the Library of Congress without a game plan—yes, it's like that, but amplified. Take it step by step. Retrieve one piece of information and spend time understanding it before diving into another one.

Practical Application of Retrieved Information

While you will find information as expansive as the universe itself, always remember to tether it to your earthly existence. That's right, the Akashic Records are not just for grand revelations about the cosmos; they offer practical advice for your day-to-day life. If you find guidance on harmonizing your inner energies, for example, don't just marvel at the esoteric wisdom. Apply it. Make it a living, breathing part of your existence.

Verifying Information

Now, this part is crucial. Just like you wouldn't accept every search result from Google as gospel truth, exercise discernment in the Akashic Records. There's a multitude of perspectives stored here. It's like a cosmic Twitter, where every entity or event has its interpretation. Cross-reference the information you retrieve with your own experience and intuitive wisdom.

So there you have it. Retrieving and interpreting information from the Akashic Records is a nuanced process, like learning to play an instrument or deciphering a complex work of art. It requires an open mind, a tuned intuition, and a methodical approach. The wisdom you unlock here can guide you in the physical world, offering insights not just into your spiritual journey, but also into the intricate dynamics of your earthly existence. Whether you're a spiritual novice or an astral traveler, the Akashic Records welcome you with layers of complexity and simplicity waiting to be explored and understood. Ah, but that's not all there is to navigating these celestial landscapes; stay with me as we go deeper into our cosmic expedition.

Limitations of the Akashic Records

"A man's got to know his limitations." Clint Eastwood, in the 1973 movie **Magnum Force**

Ah, the allure of limitless knowledge. The Akashic Records might seem like an open treasure chest, waiting for you to plunder its depths. But before you don your pirate hat, let's set some boundaries. Yes, boundaries, those contours of respect that help navigate any worthwhile relationship—even your relationship with the cosmic library known as the Akashic Records.

Your Emotional Readiness

Imagine walking into a movie theater with no age restrictions and deciding to watch a horror film as your first movie ever. You'd probably come out scarred, wouldn't you? Similarly, the Akashic Records hold information of varying emotional intensities. You may uncover life histories that include tragedies, or you may come across cosmic truths that can unsettle you. Therefore, it's important to gauge your emotional readiness before taking a deep dive into the archives. You're not here to face your fears; you're here to gather wisdom.

Time Sensitivity of Information

Think of the Akashic Records like an ever-flowing river. While the river's course remains, the water keeps moving. The information in the Records is constantly updating with each event that occurs in the universe. So, what you find today may be modified or nuanced tomorrow. Essentially, you need to take the time-sensitive nature of the Records into account. It's like checking the weather forecast; it gives you a prediction, not a guarantee.

Ethical Boundaries

The Akashic Records are not a gossip column where you get to sneak peeks into other people's lives. This cosmic library has its own ethics, believe it or not. It's like a coffee shop that trusts its patrons to pay what they think is fair. Peering into someone else's records without permission is frowned upon to put it lightly. You're not a cosmic paparazzi. You're a student in a sacred hall of learning, so maintain that decorum.

Incomplete or Fragmented Information

Ever picked up a novel to find that pages are missing or torn? While the Akashic Records are far more comprehensive than any human-made book, they might sometimes offer information that seems incomplete or fragmented. This isn't a glitch; it's often by design. There are mysteries that the human consciousness is not yet capable of comprehending. It's akin to trying to understand a complex mathematical theorem before learning basic arithmetic. Some wisdom remains beyond our grasp until we're ready for it. There are plenty of times I access a client's Akashic Records only to hit a complete blank. I then look for the client's guide and ask permission to access the records. Sometimes, I'm only given partial access. Other times I get sent away with nothing.

Reliability of Human Interpretation

Lastly, remember the game 'telephone'? One person whispers a phrase to another, and by the end of the chain, the phrase transforms entirely. Our human faculties can distort or dilute the information retrieved from the Akashic Records. We might misinterpret symbols, misunderstand metaphors, or even forget key details. Hence, while the Records themselves are trustworthy, our interpretations may not always be spot-on.

So, understanding your boundaries within the Akashic Records is less about limits and more about refining your approach. Think of it as a loving parental guide saying, "Yes, you can go out and play, but don't cross the road and stay within the neighborhood." It's not to curtail your freedom, but to enhance your experience and keep you safely within the bounds of cosmic respect and human understanding.

Remember, your journey in these celestial corridors is as much about wisdom as it is about responsibility. But now, as you better understand the contours of this sacred space, you are more prepared to explore and engage deeper, making your sojourn both enlightening and respectful. Shall we proceed?

Getting Back

In the tapestry of cosmic exploration, the departure is just as meaningful as the arrival. You've romanced the wisdom of the Akashic Records, and now it's time to dance your way back to your corporeal existence, bringing with you the treasures of newfound understanding. But how do you make that return voyage as serene and safe as your entry? Ah, the art of coming back, dear readers, is like the art of leaving a grand party; it demands finesse and a dash of style.

The Mental Bookmark

Imagine having the most enchanting conversation at a party and suddenly, you need to dash out. Wouldn't it be nice to pause, making a mental note so you can pick up right where you left off next time? The Akashic Records allow you the courtesy of mental bookmarks. As you prepare to exit, you can make a mental or spiritual 'note' about where you are in your exploration, especially if you're in the middle of something significant. This is not about stopping time, but about having a reference point to return to.

Recalling the Anchors

Your anchors are like those good friends who ensure you reach home safe after a night of merry-making. During your Akashic journey, you've set up spiritual or mental 'anchors.' These are symbols, affirmations, or even tangible items like crystals that have been imbued with the intention of grounding. Before you leave the Akashic realm, consciously connect with these anchors. It's like fastening your seatbelt before the airplane descends; it's a small but vital step in your safe return.

Gratitude and Farewell

You wouldn't leave a social gathering without a proper farewell, right? Or maybe you would, but we're talking high spiritual etiquette here. Gratitude opens doors—not just cosmic ones, but also doors within you. Taking a moment to express your gratitude to the Akashic Records, and any entities or spirits you've interacted with, seals your experience with positive energy. It's like leaving a tip at a restaurant; it's not mandatory, but it's a good practice that reflects well on you.

The Exit Visualization

Exiting the Akashic Records isn't about clicking an 'X' on a window or walking through a portal. It's more subtle, like waking up from a dream naturally without an alarm jarring you into reality. Picture your consciousness pulling back through the layers you penetrated to get here. Imagine yourself gently floating back down a celestial river, letting its currents guide you towards wakefulness. Visualize the ethereal chords connecting you to the Akashic Records slowly retracting, like the soft closing of a book you've just adored but can revisit anytime.

Physical Re-Alignment

When you're finally back, sit still for a few moments to sync your spiritual experiences with your physical body. It's like adjusting your eyes to the sunlight after coming out of a dark cinema hall. Take deep breaths, feel the earth beneath you, and touch something tangible, like a table or a wall. You're grounding your essence back into the mortal coil, solidifying your experiences from vapor to water to the ice of earthly reality.

And as you blink your eyes open, like a sleeper waking from a vivid dream, you might just find that the world looks a little different. A little brighter, a tad more mysterious, yet stunningly clearer. You've been a gallant explorer of the

Akashic Records, and now you're a humble pilgrim in the familiar yet forever-changed landscapes of your everyday life. What's next, you ask? Oh, the possibilities are endless!

CHAPTER NINE

Images and Archetypes in the Akashic Records

Accessing the Akashic Records is akin to unlocking an ancient, cosmic treasure chest. Each time you lift that lid, golden glimmers of symbols, images, and archetypes await to reveal their mysteries. They're not just there to please your aesthetic sense; they hold keys to deeper understanding and wisdom. Let's talk about how to unravel the meaning behind these visual riddles.

The Alphabet of Archetypes

You might recognize some characters when you're navigating through the Akashic Records. No, they're not pop-culture figures or people you know. They are the archetypes, the original "characters" that have existed in human psychology and culture for eons. These archetypes can appear as the Warrior, the Mother, the Sage, and so on. Each brings with them a wealth of information and significance. Think of them as the Rosetta Stone that lets you translate the language of your soul.

Portraits and Landscapes: Two Types of Images

Have you ever noticed how some photographs capture faces while others capture places? The Akashic Records can be a bit like an art gallery featuring both portraits and landscapes. Portraits generally symbolize personalities or attributes, while landscapes often relate to emotional states or life situations. For instance, a raging sea might depict turmoil, while a serene lake reflects a peaceful state of being. Learning to categorize what you're seeing helps you focus your interpretive energies more effectively.

Dynamic and Static Symbols: The Movie and the Still Image

In the Records, some symbols are like still photographs, frozen in time, while others are more like videos, full of motion and activity. The difference is crucial. Static symbols often symbolize a constant, a truth, or a situation that remains unchanged. Dynamic symbols, however, indicate ongoing processes or transformations. The key here is observation. The more you look, the more you'll understand the nature of each symbol's dynamism or lack thereof.

The Coherence of Colors

The Akashic Records don't shy away from utilizing a full palette of colors, and each hue carries its own frequency and message. For example, a symbol bathed in blue light may suggest healing or communication, while one steeped in red could indicate passion or urgency. Colors can add layers of meaning, so don't ignore them. They're not just window dressing; they're often the windows themselves.

Multi-Dimensional Meanings

Imagine reading a novel that has multiple layers of interpretation—every sentence could be taken literally, metaphorically, or allegorically. Similarly, a single symbol in the Akashic Records might possess more than one dimension of meaning. An eagle soaring in the sky could represent freedom or could hint at spiritual ascension. The layered interpretations are like different facets of a gem, each reflecting a different hue, each equally valid and beautiful.

A Web of Relations

Like in any good movie, the characters and settings in

the Akashic Records don't exist in isolation. They're interconnected, each affecting the other. The Warrior archetype standing on a mountain could signify a battle that leads to a personal summit or breakthrough. Learning to see the relationships between different symbols adds nuance to your interpretations. This isn't just a collection of individual puzzles; it's more like an intricately interwoven tapestry.

The Bridge to Consciousness

Your intuition serves as a conduit between these symbols and your conscious understanding. Treat it like a best friend who has known you forever—one who can translate the subtle nuances that you might not catch. If a symbol triggers a memory or invokes a feeling, that's your intuition acting as the interpreter. Listen carefully.

This discussion barely scratches the surface of what's possible. But as you keep revisiting your Akashic gallery, your interpretive skills will grow sharper, and the Records will start to feel less like a cryptic jigsaw puzzle and more like a beautiful story where each symbol is a word, each image a sentence, and each archetype a chapter. It's a narrative that you'll co-author with the universe, a story that's not just written in the stars but in the depths of your soul. So keep turning those pages; the next chapter promises even deeper revelations. And wouldn't you want to know what happens next?

Now What?

Sorta like the dog who chases cars and finally catches one, now what?

You've entered the Akashic Records, decoded its rich tapestry of symbols, and communed with archetypes. You're now cradling a treasure trove of wisdom, images, and understandings. But what do you do with this multifaceted jewel of cosmic information? How do you apply this ethereal knowledge to the here and now? The next step, my friends, is contextualizing.

The Importance of Personal Experience

The Akashic Records are universal, but the information gleaned from them must be applied individually. Imagine you're an artist in a studio filled with every shade of color. Your experience in the Records has just handed you a new hue. How does it fit into your existing palette? Knowing this color's unique properties enables you to incorporate it into your life's painting. Your personal experiences act as a frame, highlighting specific areas where this newfound wisdom can shine its brightest.

The Timeline as Your Canvas

As you're adding layers of cosmic understanding, it's

essential to comprehend where these insights fit in your life's timeline. Are these nuggets of wisdom relevant for your past, your present, or your future? Grasping the timing can be akin to knowing when to sow seeds in a garden. Plant too early or too late, and the harvest could be lackluster. But time it right, and you'll enjoy a bountiful yield.

Layers of Reality: The Many Floors of a Mansion

Imagine life as a grand mansion with multiple floors—each representing a different aspect of your reality. Your health, relationships, and career all have their unique rooms. As you sift through Akashic information, think about which "floor" it belongs to. If you've gained insight about healing, for example, it might directly correlate with the "health floor" of your life's mansion. Knowing where to place each piece of information helps you navigate your personal labyrinth with more finesse.

Ethereal to Earthly: The Act of Grounding

You've been flying high in the cosmic skies, and now it's time for landing. Grounding means taking that lofty knowledge and planting it firmly into your daily life. This is akin to an architect turning blueprints into a tangible structure. By crafting actionable steps, you convert metaphysical understanding into earthly benefits. Take a moment to jot down or mentally note how you can apply each Akashic insight into actionable steps.

Fusing the Universal with the Personal: Your Own Mythos

Universal truths are like stories told around a cosmic campfire. Each of us hears these tales and makes them our own. By creating your unique mythos, you become a living, breathing manifestation of your Akashic discoveries. This personal mythos is like a tree whose roots are deeply embedded in universal soil but whose branches and leaves are uniquely yours. Each leaf could be a personal story or a life lesson that's colored by the universal nutrients it's absorbed.

The Human Filter: Ego, Mind, and Emotions

While you're busy being a cosmic translator, don't forget that you're also human. Your mind, ego, and emotions will inevitably color the information you've gathered. And that's okay! Think of it as seasoning added to a dish. A pinch of your unique human qualities can make the Akashic information more palatable and applicable to your life. However, being aware of this 'seasoning' allows you to discern the original flavor of the message and how your personal taste might have altered it.

Calibration and Adjustment: Life's Control Panel

Think of your life as an elaborate control panel with knobs and dials for different sectors—health, relationships, career, and spiritual growth. As you integrate your Akashic wisdom, you'll want to adjust these settings. Perhaps you've gained insights about self-love; this would involve turning up the "relationship with self" dial. Calibration is a subtle art; tiny adjustments can make significant impacts.

Experiencing and Evaluating: The Cosmic Feedback Loop

Lastly, after you've placed the Akashic wisdom into the context of your life, it's time for the real test: living it out. As you do, you'll receive feedback—kind of like an echo in a canyon. This echo allows you to fine-tune your understanding, making your next Akashic foray even more enlightening.

As you venture further into the depths of the Akashic Records, each journey informs the next. With each trip, you don't just gather more data; you gather more of yourself. It's a never-ending spiral that doesn't just take you deeper into the Akashic mysteries, but also deeper into your own soul. And who wouldn't want to discover more of that intriguing terrain?

So, onward we go; there's so much more to explore!

You've made it this far, navigated the luminous corridors of the Akashic Records, and you're now armed with ethereal wisdom. The question looms—how to weave these celestial threads into the very fabric of your everyday life? Friends, it's time to roll up our sleeves and get practical. This isn't just about higher learning; it's about higher living. So, let's traverse these uncharted territories with your everyday concerns in hand.

Beyond Self-Help: Becoming Your Own Cosmic Advisor

The Akashic Records aren't a onetime retreat; they're an ongoing consultation service. Think of them as an expansive cosmic library that you have a lifetime membership to. For those weary of cliche self-help books, this is your personalized guide. It's like having an infinitely wise friend, always there to offer advice tailored specifically to your situation. But how do you consult this friend for daily dilemmas? You begin by phrasing your questions clearly before entering the Akashic space, like a customer walking into a consultancy firm with a well-prepared list of queries. The Akashic Records can provide solutions, ranging from career moves to relationship advice. Each time you emerge, you're not just wiser; you're more capable.

Health as a Symphony: Tuning Instruments with Akashic Insights

We all know the importance of a balanced diet, regular exercise, and mental peace. But what if the Akashic Records could provide a more nuanced understanding of your health? Think of your body as an orchestra, each organ and system playing its part. The Akashic wisdom can act as your orchestra's conductor, attuned to the cosmic score, enabling you to fine-tune individual instruments. You'll start to see your health as not merely physical but as a harmonious interplay of spiritual, emotional, and mental well-being.

Crafting a Purpose-Driven Career

You've heard the age-old adage, "Do what you love, and you'll never work a day in your life." The Akashic Records can help you go beyond mere job satisfaction to a purpose-driven career. Imagine walking into an art gallery where each painting represents a possible career path. The Akashic Records illuminate the masterpiece most aligned with your soul's journey. They can highlight overlooked talents and guide you to untapped opportunities. Your work life transforms from a daily grind into a tapestry of purpose, woven with threads of Akashic wisdom.

Relationship Alchemy: Transforming Lead into Gold

Navigating relationships can often feel like trying to solve a complex puzzle with missing pieces. This is where the Akashic Records can help you find those elusive pieces, often hidden in the corners of your own psyche. Suddenly, you're not just reacting to relationship challenges; you're understanding their cosmic rationale. Like an alchemist, you start to transform relational lead into gold. Each conflict becomes an opportunity for soul-level growth, and every connection a conduit for celestial wisdom.

Financial Abundance: Beyond Budgeting and Investing

Everyone's after the secret to financial freedom. Most self-help books regurgitate the same old advice: save more, invest wisely, budget strictly. But what if there were other, less-traveled avenues to financial abundance? The Akashic Records offer a map, drawn not just in the currency of dollars and cents, but in the more expansive currency of spiritual capital. It's as if you've discovered an entirely new way to invest, not just in stock markets but in soul markets. Investments become about energetic returns, and suddenly the universal law of give and take becomes your most reliable financial planner.

Becoming a Time-Wizard: Mastering Life's Seasons

Life ebbs and flows through different seasons. Sometimes we're in a season of growth, other times we might find ourselves in a season of rest or transformation. The Akashic Records offer a cosmic calendar, helping you understand the spiritual seasons of your life. With this knowledge, you can become a time-wizard, aligning your activities to the seasons for maximum efficacy. No more swimming against the current; you're now flowing with it, each stroke powered by Akashic insight.

Evolving as a Cosmic Citizen

Your forays into the Akashic Records have transformed you into a cosmic citizen, aware of your intergalactic duties and privileges. This consciousness makes you an asset, not just to your immediate community but to humanity as a whole. As you embrace your role as a cosmic citizen, you begin to influence those around you, gradually expanding the collective vibration of our planet.

Enriching Your Artistic Expression

Artists, writers, and musicians, listen up! The Akashic

Records aren't just libraries; they're endless art studios. Here, your art can transcend the aesthetic and touch the divine. As you channel Akashic wisdom into your creations, you'll find they resonate on a frequency that's soul-stirring, not just eye-catching. Each stroke, each word, each note becomes a loving caress from the universe to the souls who engage with your work.

So, with the Akashic Records as your guide, every facet of life shines brighter, resonates deeper, and carries within it a slice of the divine. You become not just an earthly being having a spiritual experience, but a celestial being mastering the art of earthly living. And so, dear friends, as we expand our understanding, let's not forget to revel in the pure joy of our cosmic adventures. After all, it's not just about the destination; it's about the soul-enriching journey that keeps calling us back for more.

Healing and Spiritual Growth

So, you've unlocked the cosmic vault of the Akashic Records, brushed against ethereal wisdom and glimpsed sacred scrolls. Your spirit is buoyant with newfound knowledge, but you're also brimming with questions. You may wonder, "Can the Akashic Records actually heal me? Can they spark a spiritual renaissance within my soul?"

These questions point us toward an essential exploration of how to use the Akashic wisdom for both healing and profound spiritual growth. We're not talking about Band-Aid solutions or superficial awakenings. Oh no, we're treading on sacred ground where the very roots of your existence meet the divine soil. Let's tread carefully but boldly, shall we?

Mending the Invisible Wounds: Emotional Healing

Imagine your emotional traumas as a dark cloud looming overhead. Instead of dispersing, it keeps gathering more weight, casting shadows over your happiness. The Akashic Records can act like a sunbeam, piercing through this dark cloud and evaporating the lingering emotional weight. You'll find that as you venture deeper into the Akashic wisdom, the dark clouds of trauma and anxiety begin to lose their grip. What remains is the clear sky of emotional freedom, offering you an expansive view of endless possibilities.

Rejuvenating the Mortal Coil: Physical Healing

Now, let's consider your physical body as a temple, perhaps a bit tarnished from years of neglect or environmental exposure. As you walk through the Akashic hallways, you find that each step is a stroke of the divine craftsman's chisel, taking off a layer of tarnish. This is not a promise of an overnight miracle cure but a journey towards wellness that transcends pills and medical jargon. We're talking about vibrant health that springs from a soul-deep well of cosmic equilibrium.

Nurturing the Blossom of the Soul: Individual Growth

Ever felt like you're meant for something more but can't quite put your finger on it? Consider your soul a seed, silently crying out to break through the soil and reach toward the sun. With the Akashic Records, you are granted the perfect conditions to help this seed sprout, grow, and finally bloom. The Records offer insights into your deepest desires and potential, thereby fertilizing your spiritual soil with nutrients for the soul's blossoming.

Orchestrating Harmony: Relational Growth

Relationships are complicated, no doubt about it. Think of them as multi-faceted crystals, beautiful but intricate, with every surface reflecting a different color. Akashic wisdom enables you to understand the intricacies of these emotional crystals. It can guide you in offering love, grace, and understanding, not just to others but to yourself. A spiritual lesson doesn't only involve your solitary path; it also includes your connections, your community, and even the collective consciousness.

Piercing Through the Veil: Increasing Intuitive Abilities

Many of us intuit that a sixth sense lingers within, whispering truths that the five physical senses can't grasp. Imagine your intuition as a dormant volcano, teeming with the potential to light up the night sky. Akashic insights work as the seismic shift that can awaken this dormant power, making your intuitive perceptions erupt like a spectacular natural phenomenon. This newly heightened intuition is like an internal GPS system finely tuned to the cosmic frequencies.

Navigating Karmic Cycles: Clearing Ancestral and Past-Life Baggage

We're all entangled in a web of actions and reactions, spanning across lifetimes and even trickling down from our ancestors. Consider these karmic cycles as a complex maze. The Akashic Records serve as your personal guide, helping you navigate this labyrinth. They point out where you have been running in circles and show you the exit route, freeing you to explore new landscapes of experience.

Scaling Cosmic Peaks: Achieving Enlightenment

Don't think of enlightenment as a far-off mountain peak, visible but eternally distant. With the Akashic Records, it becomes a mountain you are already scaling, step by transformative step. Every lesson learned, every piece of wisdom integrated, serves as a climbing gear, helping you ascend this lofty peak. While the summit may not be immediately within reach, the joy is in the climb, in the discovery of new vistas of consciousness along the way.

What unfolds through this journey is not just healing or growth in isolated pockets of your life, but an all-encompassing, soul-deep transformation. The pieces of the cosmic puzzle fall into place, not only making you whole, but also a wholesomely radiant being, inside and out.

As we flow through this stream of cosmic wisdom, we see our reflections in its sparkling water—not as we think we should be, but as we truly are: Divine beings, capable of healing and boundless spiritual growth. And as we step onto the banks of this celestial river, we realize that it branches into many directions, each offering a new adventure of soulful proportions. One of these branches might lead us to discover how to manifest this sacred knowledge into tangible, day-to-day actions. Shall we venture further?

Ethical Considerations

Of course, there's more on this. It's important and bears repeating. Before you make a headlong dash into the pulsating vortex of the Akashic Records, let's unfurl the scroll of ethics—equally glittering with wisdom but much less talked about. Indeed, the road to the Akashic Records is not just about imbibing celestial wisdom like nectar; it's also about understanding how to handle this nectar with care. Think of it as coming upon an ancient treasure chest; it's not just the gleam of gold and jewels that matters, but also how responsibly you handle your newfound wealth.

Respect the Records: It's Not a Game

Let's imagine the Akashic Records as the most exclusive library you've ever entered. The air is thick with sanctity, and the guardians of this domain don't take their roles lightly. This is not a realm for idle curiosity or gossip. Treat your visit as you would a sacred pilgrimage. Just as you wouldn't desecrate a holy site, don't misuse the Akashic wisdom for petty intrigues.

The Information Is Not Yours Alone: Respecting Privacy

Think of the Akashic Records as a spiritual internet where privacy settings are far more serious. Just because you can access someone's records doesn't mean you should. Would you rifle through a friend's diary without permission? Unlikely, I hope. The same principle applies here; always seek consent if your inquiries concern someone else. Respecting boundaries is not just ethical; it's divine etiquette.

Balance of Power: Avoid Manipulation

A subtle point, but a crucial one. When you can read the unwritten and perceive the hidden, the balance of power shifts in your favor. Imagine you're at a poker table, and you suddenly develop the ability to see everyone's cards. Tempting as it may be to profit from this edge, remember that the Akashic Records are not a cheat sheet for life. Use your wisdom to guide, heal, and assist—never to manipulate or dominate.

Intent Matters: Use for Good, Not Harm

Visualize a glass of water. On its own, it's neutral—it can quench thirst or, if thrown with force, can startle or even hurt someone. The Akashic wisdom is that glass of water; your intent determines its impact. Your reasons for accessing the Records should align with positive outcomes. Be honest with yourself. If your intention leans toward harming others or yourself, reconsider your motives and realign with a more virtuous path.

Accountability: Own the Consequences

The moment you step into the Akashic vault, you become an ethereal alchemist, capable of transformative feats. But even alchemists must take responsibility for the potions they brew. Imagine your actions as stones tossed into a still lake, sending ripples far and wide. You might not see where the ripples reach, but rest assured, they go farther than you think. Always remember, with great power comes, yes, you guessed it, great responsibility.

Silence Is Golden: Discretion

This point can't be emphasized enough. What you learn from the Akashic Records is not always for public display. You're not a spiritual tabloid journalist, breaking exclusive scoops on people's past lives or future probabilities. Treat what you learn as confidential. Of course, if the information can help someone and you have their permission, by all means, share— but do it judiciously and respectfully.

Honoring The Process: No Shortcuts

You may feel like a cosmic voyager, eager to jet off into the Akashic cosmos. But shortcuts in this spiritual journey are often illusions, or worse, traps. Skipping steps or rushing through rituals not only dilutes your experience, but might also risk the safety of your spiritual expedition. It's like driving on a winding mountain road; cutting corners could mean a perilous fall.

Navigating through these ethical considerations is akin

to learning how to wield a sword. A sword can be a weapon of destruction or a tool for justice. Its impact depends not on the sword itself but on the hands that wield it. As you attune yourself to these ethical vibrations, you begin to resonate with the divine integrity that forms the bedrock of the Akashic Records.

In this rich tapestry of wisdom, these threads of ethical considerations may seem less glittering than others, yet they're crucial for maintaining the fabric's integrity. They make sure you're not just a passive reader but an engaged, responsible contributor to this celestial repository.

And now, while we're attuned to the frequency of ethical awareness, let's turn our gaze toward another facet of this diamond-like domain. What might it mean to become a lifelong student of the Akashic Records? Ah, but that's another tale, offering its own blend of riddles and revelations. Shall we journey on?

CHAPTER TEN

Ah, my cosmic traveler, your steps have led you to a threshold few dare approach: mastering the enigmatic dance of time within the Akashic Records. When it comes to this endeavor, time is not merely a river; it's an ever-shifting sea, a tapestry woven from myriad threads, each one representing a unique moment in existence. To master time manipulation within this sacred dimension is akin to learning how to navigate not just the Earth's oceans, but those of different planets and dimensions. Exciting, is it not?

The Illusory Nature of Time

First and foremost, it's vital to grasp that time within the Akashic Records doesn't operate like the ticking clock on your wall or the calendar on your device. No, time here is more like a chameleon—changeable, fluid, adapting to the observer's perceptions. Picture it this way: instead of walking along a straight road where you can only go forward or back, imagine that you're on a spherical surface. You can move in any direction, circling around to cross your own path from a different angle. Start wrapping your head around this, and you've taken the first step toward mastery.

The Wisdom of Synchronicity

Let's talk about the term 'synchronicity,' coined by Carl Jung, which is quite apropos in this context. You know how sometimes, out of the blue, you think of someone you haven't seen in years and then bump into them the very next day? That's a low-level brush with synchronicity. When you're within the Akashic Records, you can actively tap into this phenomenon, opening yourself up to 'coincidences' that are more like cosmic winks. These alignments allow you to recognize when and where to act, or not to act, within the tapestry of time.

Quantum Leaps: Future and Past Projections

Within the Records, the future and the past coalesce in intriguing ways, offering not just glimpses but full, vivid experiences of both. Imagine you're watching a film but can slip into the screen and live the scenes, feeling all the emotions, sensing all the textures. Now translate this to your own life's movie; you can project yourself into past or future events with crystal clarity. These projections are not mere daydreams. They are energetic forays that can influence your real-world actions and decisions.

Revisiting and Revising Past Moments

We've all had moments we wish we could redo. What if I told you that within the Akashic Records, this is more than a whimsical notion? You can return to past choices and explore the path not taken. Picture it like editing a manuscript; you can't change the already-published book, but you can gain new insights and perspectives that enrich the chapters yet to be written. This is no game of make-believe; it's a powerful form of spiritual 'revisionism,' impacting your soul at profound levels.

Tachyons and the Speed of Time

Ever been so engrossed in a task that time flew by, or so bored that it crawled? That's time's relativity at play in our daily lives. Within the Akashic Records, you'll come across tachyons—hypothetical particles that move faster than light. Your interaction with these tachyons can warp your perception of time, allowing you to stretch or compress your experiences.

It's like having a magical remote control that can fast-forward, rewind, or pause time. Why is this useful, you ask? Well, imagine soaking in centuries of wisdom in what feels like just minutes.

Creating Temporal Landmarks

Remember the breadcrumbs Hansel and Gretel used to mark their way? Consider creating your own breadcrumbs in the Akashic Records, but not to find your way back; instead, you're establishing temporal landmarks for quicker access to specific moments or experiences. Think of it as bookmarking a website for quick future reference, but in this case, you're bookmarking moments in the cosmic continuum. This is vital for when you wish to delve deeper into a past revelation or when you need to accelerate your understanding of upcoming events.

So, dear soul traveler, I bet you're itching to try out these time tricks and treats within the Records. But remember, mastery comes not just from understanding the techniques, but also from embodying the wisdom and ethics that govern their use. The time you invest in grasping these profound aspects of the Akashic Records is not just mere minutes and hours; it's an immortal footprint on the spiraling pathway of your soul's journey.

Is your mind buzzing with possibilities? I thought so.

Now, having explored time's malleability, how about we segue into something even more tantalizing: mastering the language of Light that encodes the Akashic Records themselves? But ah, let's save that delectable subject for another sublime moment, shall we? The universe, after all, has all the time in the world for us to explore its secrets.

Deepening your Relationship with Hermes/Thoth

Ah, you find yourself now standing at the altar of wisdom, yearning to commune with Hermes—or as the ancient Egyptians called him, Thoth—the guardian of esoteric knowledge and the cosmic scribe. We are venturing into an extraordinarily sacred partnership, a relationship that goes beyond mere intellectual pursuits, plunging deep into the waters of the soul. Let your spirit be steeled and your mind opened wide, for we are about to explore avenues that even the bravest travelers might hesitate to tread.

Your First Encounter

Remember your initial experience with Hermes/Thoth, that mysterious, intoxicating moment when you felt the brush of something grand against your psyche? That was more than simple fascination; it was the seed of a divine relationship being planted. Like the first time a musician picks up their destined instrument and feels an inexplicable connection, your first encounter with Hermes/Thoth was the universe's serenade, a love song of wisdom and secrets.

The Caduceus Code: Symbols and Signs

Surely, you've seen his emblematic staff, the Caduceus, with intertwined serpents spiraling around a winged rod. This isn't mere ornamentation. Think of it as a barcode, a condensed summary of his multifaceted character. When you meditate on this symbol, you're connecting with layers upon layers of ancient wisdom—alchemy, duality, transformation, and more. Imagine being a novelist who stumbles upon an old, tattered book with fables you've never read; each page unravels new ideas, new characters, and new worlds to explore.

The Whisperings: Signs and Omens

Hermes/Thoth doesn't communicate like your chatty neighbor. Oh no, his whispers manifest as symbols, recurring thoughts, even peculiar events that seem randomly juxtaposed—until you realize they're not. Take note of these signs; they're celestial texts and need to be deciphered. Consider each a phrase in an ongoing conversation with the deity. For instance, if you suddenly find feathers on your path or hear the same phrase repeated throughout your day from multiple sources, stop and reflect; Hermes/Thoth might be sending you a message.

The Book of Thoth: Arcane Studies

This ancient text, also known as the Tarot, is an esoteric tool intimately linked to Thoth. Learning the language of Tarot is like becoming fluent in Hermes/Thoth's sacred dialect. Think of it this way: instead of using words, you're expressing thoughts and queries through a deck of cards, each one a syllable in a divine conversation. When you lay the cards, you're speaking; when you interpret them, you're listening. It's an intimate dialog that transcends mere words.

Dreamwalking with Hermes

In ancient Greece, seekers of wisdom would sleep in Hermes' temples to receive divine messages. You can bring this practice into your modern life by setting an intention before sleep to meet Hermes in your dreams. You see, dreams are an unrestricted playground for the gods. It's as if you're extending an invitation for a tête-à-tête in a celestial café, one that exists between the folds of reality and imagination. The encounters here might be symbolic or direct, but each is a nectar drop of divine revelation.

Sharing the Cup: Rituals and Offerings

Fostering a relationship with Hermes/Thoth isn't a one-way street. Just as you wouldn't show up empty-handed to a friend's dinner party, you should consider offerings and rituals as your contributions to this celestial friendship. Picture yourself sipping an aged whiskey with a beloved mentor; that's the essence of sharing an offering with Hermes/Thoth. It could be as simple as lighting a lavender candle or as complex as performing a moonlit ritual involving esoteric symbols and incantations.

Synchronizing Frequencies: Chanting and Mantras

As you become more attuned to Hermes/Thoth, the need will arise to match his higher vibrational frequency. Think of it as tuning an old radio until you find the station where the signal is crystal clear. The use of chants, prayers, or mantras dedicated to him serves this purpose. Each syllable you utter acts as a stepping-stone, constructing an energetic bridge between your essence and his.

Now then, are you feeling the weight of your soul lightening, perhaps a tingling of anticipation rippling across your consciousness? That's the thrill of spiritual camaraderie, my friend. As we peel back the veils, the journey inward gets increasingly fascinating, deeper, more significant, revealing chambers of our soul previously hidden even from ourselves.

But let's not allow the sheer thrill of this newfound connection sweep us off our feet just yet. We must understand the other techniques that go hand in hand with such mastery— like the shaping of cosmic energy into tangible forms. Ah, but we're getting ahead of ourselves. More on that tantalizing subject will follow; rest assured, Hermes/Thoth has much more to unveil, in time, with your continued commitment. Shall we proceed?

Group Akashic Work

Ah, the allure of group Akashic journeys, an experience akin to embarking on an epic adventure with a fellowship of kindred souls. Imagine you and your companions are like a troupe of explorers setting sail for uncharted waters, navigating by the constellations of ancient wisdom above you. Each one of you has a purpose, a role, a special gift to bring into this shared mystical venture. It's more than an expedition; it's a symphony where each individual's intuitive tune adds to the grand cosmic melody. So let's set the stage, shall we?

Crafting the Akashic Circle

You wouldn't set out on an adventure without knowing your companions, right? The same applies to an Akashic journey. The first point to consider is the selection of participants. The chosen few must resonate on similar frequencies, a gathering of souls like tuning forks vibrating in harmony. A discordant note could distort the energy flow. Picture it as a campfire storytelling night; each participant is a crucial log in that fire. One wet log can disrupt the entire circle.

The Nexus: A Shared Entry Point

Imagine you're all standing before a majestic library. Instead of an ordinary entrance, you have several. Each door is an option, a different style and age, much like the myriad paths one can choose to reach the Akashic Records. The nexus is the shared entry point your group agrees upon, a focal vision or symbolism. As you collectively focus on this shared door, you amplify each other's intent and energy, making the portal vibrant and more accessible.

Synchronized Intention Setting

Visualize this: a chorus of voices singing different songs would create a cacophony. To work in harmony, you must all sing the same tune. Before accessing the Records, set a group intention. It could be for healing, understanding, or even solving a problem that has stumped you all. This united intention acts as an anchor, stabilizing your journey and ensuring the collective energies are attuned for a specific purpose.

The Silent Conductor: Designating a Guide

In a chamber orchestra, musicians look towards the conductor for cues. Similarly, in a group Akashic journey, it's wise to have a designated guide. This person functions as the navigator, steering the group through the Records, ensuring focus is maintained and assisting if any disturbances occur. The guide's role is not to control but to facilitate. Picture a seasoned captain steering a ship through turbulent waters, knowing when to push ahead and when to adapt the course.

The Akashic Dialog

As you traverse the halls of this cosmic library, you may encounter ancestral spirits, archetypal symbols, or unspoken wisdom. How does one interpret these for a group? Think of it as a shared dream. Each individual deciphers what they perceive and share it with the group. These interpretations are pieced together, much like a puzzle, offering a composite understanding that's more multi-faceted than what any individual would perceive alone.

Grounding Rituals: The Return

Ah, the journey back is equally important. When astronauts return to Earth, they go through a re-entry process to adapt to the planet's atmosphere. Similarly, a grounding ritual serves to ease the transition back into everyday consciousness. Think of it as gently waking up from a deep, collective dream. A simple ritual, like jointly extinguishing a ceremonial candle, can act as the wake-up call, signaling the journey's end yet preserving the sacred experience.

Reflect and Digest: Post-Journey Discussion

After your Akashic sailing is done, don't just pack up your compasses and astrolabes. Discuss. Reflect. Share. Imagine having watched a breathtaking movie with friends; you'd want to talk about it, wouldn't you? In a similar fashion, each participant shares their insights and the messages they received. This reflection time enriches the overall experience, giving everyone an opportunity to glimpse the journey through each other's eyes.

Because things can be a lot more fun with groups! Imagine being the only person at a sporting event. That'd be boring. Allow a bunch of friends to join in, everyone is having a grand time.

Although, sometimes things can get in the way. As we'll see next.

Dealing with Potential Obstacles

Ah, the concept of obstacles. Just as in the grand story

of any hero's journey, challenges and roadblocks are inevitable. Imagine you're setting out to explore a dense, mystical forest, much like the fabled realms of Avalon or Yggdrasil. You'd expect twisted paths, unexpected detours, and perhaps even a rogue trickster here and there, wouldn't you? Yet, these obstacles aren't mere hindrances; they are often cryptic clues or tests of mettle, designed to deepen your relationship with the Akashic Records. With that poetic prelude, let us venture forth.

Recognizing Illusory Barriers

First on our list is the recognition of false obstructions or illusory barriers. These could be as subtle as a distracting thought that drifts into your mind or as vivid as a daunting mental image. Picture yourself in a labyrinth. Some walls seem impassable, but when you touch them, your hand goes right through! It's your own inner challenges and fears masquerading as barriers. Recognizing these illusions for what they are is your first step towards outwitting them.

Confronting Personal Shadows

Ah, the shadows that lurk within each of us! Much like the unexpected appearance of a wolf on your forest journey, the encounter can be intimidating. Yet, this wolf represents your own suppressed emotions or unresolved issues. In such situations, the key isn't to run away or engage in battle. Instead, acknowledging its presence and even learning from it can transform the wolf into a guide, revealing hidden depths within the Akashic Records and within yourself.

The Lure of Ego Gratification

The glittering allure of the ego can be as mesmerizing as a siren's call. When you stumble upon information that strokes your ego—say, an impression that you were someone famous in a past life—tread cautiously. The siren's song is enticing but often leads to rocky shores. Ask yourself, "Is this serving my higher learning, or is it merely a self-aggrandizing fantasy?" As captivating as it might be to follow the siren's melody, remember that the ego often distorts the true essence of the Records.

Preservation of Free Will: No Spoilers Allowed!

Venturing deeper into your forest, you find a magical pond. It shows you glimpses of the future, but they are hazy, incomplete. The Akashic Records respect the sanctity of free will. You may find indications of possible future paths, but it's crucial to remember that these are not set in stone. Picture it as a choose-your-own-adventure book; you still hold the pen.

The Never-Ending Rabbit Hole

You've heard people talk about doing down a rabbit hole. I do it almost weekly on video channels. And that can happen when visiting the awesome libraries of the Akashic Records. As you navigate this mystical world, each discovery could lead you down another corridor of questions, much like a never-ending rabbit hole. The abundance of information can be overwhelming, like finding a treasure chest and not knowing which gem to examine first. However, overindulgence may drain your energies, diluting your focus. Knowing when to pause and digest your discoveries is an essential skill to master.

Maintaining Vibrational Integrity

Think of this as keeping your torch aflame in a gusty environment. Your vibrational state needs to be protected when accessing the Records, as it's susceptible to external influences. Imagine your energy as a glowing sphere around you; any hole in that sphere can leak energy, affecting your experience. Sealing these gaps requires mindful intention, ensuring that your vibrational integrity remains undistorted.

Detaching from Expectations

As our journey winds down, the last point to ponder is

detachment from expectations. You might enter the Akashic Records with preconceived notions about what you'll find. However, clinging to these can act like blinders, restricting your view. It's like walking through the forest, expecting to find a unicorn, and overlooking the pixies, nymphs, and other magical creatures around you. Detach, let go, and allow the Records to unfold their wisdom in their own magnificent way.

Oh, the thrill of navigating through these potential obstacles is nothing short of exhilarating, wouldn't you agree? They add layers to your Akashic quest, making it as enriching as it is enlightening. Every twist and turn holds a lesson, and each lesson is a jewel waiting to be discovered. Feel that tingling sensation of suspense? That's your soul's way of saying it's excited for what's coming next. Yes, the journey continues, and so does our saga. Onward, shall we?

Enhancing the Clarity and Depth of Your Akashic Experiences

Navigating Through the Fog of Akashic Uncertainty

Picture your entry into the Akashic Records as a voyage across an endless ocean under a mystical moonlit sky. The waters may be calm, the journey serene, but occasionally, you'll encounter mist, fog, or a churning sea that blurs your vision. Now, isn't the real adventure in piercing through that fog, to make your ethereal experiences as vibrant as a painter's most vivid masterpiece? Absolutely! Let's set sail and explore how to enhance the clarity and depth of your Akashic journey.

Establishing A Point of Entry

As any seasoned explorer will tell you, where you begin your expedition makes all the difference. It's like the difference between starting at the edge of a forest and entering through a well-defined trail. Your point of entry should be familiar, comfortable, and filled with a sense of wonder. Perhaps it's a mythical garden or a sacred temple from your dreams. By beginning at this spot, you cultivate a point of stability and safety that anchors your Akashic voyage.

Symbolic Anchors

Once you're at sea, navigators use constellations to find their way. In the Akashic Records, symbols can act as your North Star. Whether it's an ancient sigil, a power animal, or a sacred geometry shape, aligning with a symbolic anchor not only acts as a guide but can also enhance the depth of your experience. This symbol should be something that resonates with your very core, a graphical essence that unites you with the infinite.

Mindful Intention-Setting

The intentions you set are the winds that propel your sails. Setting a focused intention before accessing the Records is much like choosing a specific route before embarking on a grand adventure. It narrows down the countless possibilities and brings into focus the information and experiences that are most relevant to you. Make your intention specific but not narrow, kind of like aiming for a particular cluster of islands instead of just 'due east.'

Pre-Akashic Rituals

You wouldn't set sail without checking your equipment or consulting your maps, would you? Pre-Akashic rituals such as grounding exercises, candle-lit invocations, or a spoken prayer can tune your spiritual frequency and prepare you for deeper exploration. Think of these rituals as rolling out a plush, red carpet for your soul, paving the way for an elevated experience.

The Art of Receptivity

A true mariner learns not just to sail but to listen—to the winds, the tides, even the distant cry of a seagull. In the Akashic Records, learning to be receptive means quieting your thoughts and allowing the information to flow into you. It's akin to opening your sails fully to catch the wind; the more you can do this, the faster and further you can explore.

Trusting Your Intuition Over Logic

In navigating these cosmic waters, you must trust your intuition as much as your compass. Our logical mind tends to filter out messages or symbols that don't make immediate sense. However, your gut feeling often perceives the deeper currents that your rational mind might overlook. Just like sometimes you have to sail against the wind to make headway, you may need to go against conventional logic to grasp the profound wisdom of the Records.

Vibrational Alignment and Attunements

The frequency you operate on can either clarify or distort the Akashic experiences. Imagine if you could adjust the frequency of your ship's radio to catch a mysterious broadcast. You could say this is similar to vibrational alignments or attunements, where practices like Reiki, sound bathing, or chakra balancing can fine-tune your vibrational state, preparing you for clearer Akashic communications.

The Power of Repetition

Revisiting the Records is like circumnavigating your ocean of interest over and over, each time learning to ride new currents and discovering hidden treasures. Every journey further familiarizes you with the landscape, making each subsequent trip richer and more enlightening. Don't be a one-time tourist; become a seasoned explorer.

Narrating or Journaling Your Experiences

As a seasoned explorer, you'd keep a travel log, right? Narrating or journaling your Akashic experiences as they occur—or immediately after—helps solidify them in your consciousness. It's like etching the outline of a new island you discovered onto your sea chart. The more details you can capture, the more vivid your cognitive map becomes for future expeditions.

Post Akashic Integration

Finally, what good is discovering a new island if you don't take the time to explore it thoroughly, or in this case, integrate your newfound wisdom into your daily life? Once you 'dock back' into your regular consciousness, take the time to reflect on your experiences, to ponder the symbols, messages, or lessons you've received. This is how you translate ethereal wisdom into tangible growth.

Ah, can you feel it? The wind in your sails, the salt on your lips, the thrill of uncharted waters? That's your soul yearning for the next voyage, eager for the untold depths yet to be discovered. Each point here is not just a tool but a promise—

a promise of richer landscapes, of deeper truths, and of a more vibrant connection with the Records. The endless ocean calls; will you answer? The moonlight dances on the water's surface, as if winking at you, inviting you for the next leg of our grand adventure.

CHAPTER ELEVEN

The Final Scroll: Unraveling the Threads of a Cosmic Tapestry

Ah, the finale! You've weathered storms and navigated through the astral seas of the Akashic Records. Your soul has surfed the cosmic waves, touched the corners of universal wisdom, and here we are, at the closing chapter—but not the end, my friends, just another beginning. Before we part ways, let's revisit the magical mosaic we've pieced together.

Understanding the Pre-Entry Phase

Think of this phase as the moment you pack your bags before a trip. What you pack and how you prepare sets the tone for the whole journey. Remember the emphasis on grounding techniques, intention setting, and choosing an entry point? That's your cosmic travel kit. Be it a meditation or an invocation, how you approach the Akashic door matters. It's like knocking respectfully before entering someone's house; you prepare the space and yourself for what's coming.

Sacred Geometry and Power Symbols

The compass and map of our Akashic travels! Just like stars guided ancient mariners, sacred geometry and symbols—your personal mandalas or archetypes—serve as your navigational tools in the Akashic sea. They don't just point the way; they harmonize your being with the greater cosmic symphony.

Importance of Intuition and Receptivity

In an echoing cave, you can't hear your own voice if you keep shouting. There's a fine balance between asking questions and receiving answers in the Akashic domain. Open your sails to the wisdom winds, let go of preconceived notions and allow the Records to speak through symbols, feelings, or even words. Remember, your intuition is your first mate, always by your side, guiding you when charts fail.

Anchoring in the Astral: Creating Your Sacred Space

Much like a space traveler would need a home base on

a distant planet, you need your anchor point in the Akashic space. A temple, a garden, or perhaps a cosmic library—this is your safe haven where you can retreat to, assimilate your experiences, and collect your thoughts.

The Essence of Questions

Ah, questions are the winds that push your vessel. Your inquiries must be as precise as a jeweler's cut, yet as open-ended as the sky, inviting multifaceted wisdom. After all, a well-aimed arrow not only hits the target but also reveals what lies beyond!

Navigating with Purpose and Freedom

You've asked the right questions, but don't be tethered by them. Be open to cosmic detours. If your exploration reveals an interesting side path, why not take it? The Records are not a linear archive but a multi-dimensional field. You are both the wanderer and the cartographer of this celestial expanse.

Rituals and Vibrational Attunements

Your soul's tuning fork! Whether it's sound bathing, essential oils, or energy work, these techniques help align your vibrational frequencies to the Records. Think of it as fine-tuning a radio to catch a faraway station; you don't want static when wisdom is being broadcasted.

Navigating Group Journeys

Ah, the excitement of a group expedition! When venturing into the Akashic Records with others, be aware of the collective energy. Like a chorus, every voice matters, and a single off-key note can alter the harmony. Collective intentions, shared symbols, and mutual trust amplify the experience manifold.

The Reality of Obstacles and Shadows

Just as a treasure map has its perilous territories marked by a skull and crossbones, the Akashic Records have their own challenges. Your fears, doubts, or unresolved issues can act as fog or turbulent waters. Recognizing and confronting them is as crucial as reading the stars for direction.

Journaling and the Art of Cosmic Cartography

Don't be content with being a passive passenger; become the chronicler of your own odyssey. Documenting your encounters, impressions, and received wisdom gives shape to the nebulous. Your journal becomes a hand-drawn map for future expeditions, refined with each new journey.

Integration and Life Application

Like spices bought from a distant land, the insights and wisdom from the Akashic Records add flavor to your earthly life. This is not a realm you visit and leave; it's an eternal wellspring you carry within you. By consciously integrating what you've learned, you turn wisdom into transformation, making the Akashic experience not just a journey but a way of life.

As we close this chapter, I want you to imagine holding a gleaming golden key. This key doesn't lock away the wisdom you've gained but rather opens countless more doors. There's a universe brimming with untapped potential, swirling around you like a galaxy waiting to be explored. As we bring our current voyage to a tranquil harbor, remember: countless oceans of cosmic wisdom still beckon. Ahoy, cosmic voyager, your next adventure awaits! Are you ready?

The Golden Quill: Why Hermes/Thoth is Your Cosmic Librarian

As we stand on the shore, gazing back at the infinite ocean of Akashic wisdom we've voyaged through, a solitary figure emerges from the mists—Hermes or Thoth, if you like to keep it old school. Let's not hastily dismiss him as just another deity in the cosmic roll-call. Ah, he's far more! He's your personal librarian, your tour guide, and the guardian of sacred mysteries. Let's unravel the layers of his enigmatic existence.

Guardian of the Akashic Threshold

Imagine standing before a grand, ornate door. The key is in your hand, but do you dare to open it? This is where Hermes swoops in, as if riding the winds. His ethereal presence reassures your soul. Hermes is the keeper of thresholds, doorways, and transitions. He's like the bouncer at an exclusive, celestial club; you're getting in because you're on the list—the list of seekers, that is.

Messenger Between Worlds

Hermes doesn't merely live in one dimension; he flits effortlessly between the worlds like a hummingbird between flowers. He's the ultimate cosmic courier. Having a deity who understands the vernacular of both mortals and immortals is a gift that keeps on giving. Imagine texting someone who translates your jargon into soulful wisdom and cosmic insights; that's Hermes for you. He plays the celestial go-between when you're stumbling over cosmic syntax.

Purveyor of the Sacred Arts

Picture this: a grand celestial library where every word

ever thought or spoken is recorded. You might get lost among the endless shelves, but Hermes? He knows where each book rests. Hermes empowers your rituals and incantations, adding that dash of divine oomph. It's like discovering a hidden cheat code in a complex video game, giving you access to untold possibilities.

A Confidant in Spiritual Crisis

Embarking on a spiritual journey is no walk in the park. Sometimes the glaring cosmic sun blinds you, or you trip over spiritual pebbles. You wonder: What's the point? Hermes comes along, offers a celestial wink and says, "I get it." Just knowing that an immortal being understands your struggles can ignite your spirit like a phoenix rising from the ashes.

The Conductor of Synchronicities

Ah, the small magical moments that are not so small. Found a feather on your path right after asking the Universe for a sign? That's Hermes sprinkling his dose of enchantment in your life. He orchestrates these synchronicities like a master conductor, ensuring each note of your life blends into a symphony of significance.

As you saunter down this winding path of spiritual illumination, it's comforting to have a companion as multifaceted as Hermes or Thoth. This deity doesn't just hold the lantern as you navigate through the misty terrains of the Akashic Records; he illuminates your very soul. He's that captivating book you can't put down, the song you can't get out of your head, and the story that becomes a part of you.

But remember, this isn't a mere epilogue; it's an invitation for sequels, unwritten chapters, and uncharted cosmic territories. Hermes beckons you to continue this extraordinary journey. Take his hand, feel the electric charge of limitless possibilities, and step boldly into the next exhilarating chapter of your cosmic narrative. Your spirit's inkwell is eternally full, and the quill? Oh, it's pure gold!

The Cosmic Suitcase: Your Essential Checklist for Future Akashic Explorations

You wouldn't dare embark on a worldly adventure without packing the essentials, would you? Much like your favorite multi-pocketed carry-on, your spiritual journey into the Akashic Records demands a well-curated checklist. These aren't just items; they're lifelines, invisible strings pulling you ever-closer to the celestial nexus of wisdom. Let's zip open that cosmic suitcase and see what's inside.

The Master Key: Intention

Ah, the cornerstone of all quests—Intention. Don't mistake it for a simple thought or a fleeting wish. This is your compass, your North Star. Remember the saying, "where attention goes, energy flows"? That's your intention right there, creating an energetic tether between you and your chosen record. It's your first handshake with the Universe, so make it a firm one.

The Cosmic Passport: Rituals

Any travel-savvy person knows the importance of having their documents in order. Your ritual acts as your cosmic passport and visa. This might range from lighting a particular incense to a series of affirmations, even to the intricacy of drawing sacred symbols. Rituals ground your physical being as your spiritual self soars high. Think of it as your safety belt while your soul takes flight.

Energetic Snacks: Crystals and Talismans

Ever gone hiking without a snack? Doesn't work out too well, does it? In the case of Akashic explorations, crystals and talismans are your energetic munchies. Rose quartz, amethyst, or perhaps a custom talisman infused with your energy—these aren't just shiny objects. They act as batteries, holding and radiating energy that sustains you during your journey. Picture them as cosmic granola bars, there to nourish you when you need a little extra oomph.

Your Trusty Map: Visualization

The mind's eye is more potent than you think. Like a treasure map scrawled in celestial ink, your power of visualization guides you to the crux of your Akashic voyage. Having a clear mental image not only aids in accessing the records but also in decoding them. Imagine having Google Maps while Marco Polo had only the stars and intuition; you're that much ahead of the game!

The Return Ticket: Grounding Exercises

Your spiritual sojourns may be exhilarating, but what's equally crucial is the landing. Think of grounding exercises as your return ticket, ensuring you arrive back in your body safe, sound, and integrated. This could be anything from deep breathing to simply touching the earth with your bare feet, a gentle reminder that your physical existence is just as celestial as your cosmic one.

These checkpoints aren't mere accessories; they're essentials. Intention, rituals, talismans, visualization, and grounding—each serves a unique, indispensable purpose in your Akashic expeditions. It's like going on a safari; you wouldn't leave without your binoculars and field guide, would you? Each time you venture into the Akashic plains, this cosmic checklist ensures you're not just a wanderer but a well-equipped explorer.

So go ahead, take this checklist, tuck it into your heart, and let it be the pocket guide for your soul's eternal journey. After all, the Akashic Records aren't just a destination, but a continuum—ever-expanding, just like you. Feel that tingling anticipation? That's your spirit, already flipping through the first page of its next grand adventure.

The Cosmic Library Card: Your Guide to Further Resources and Reading

Ah, you've arrived at this phase of your Akashic journey! It's akin to having tasted a spoonful of ambrosia and now yearning to devour the entire feast. Worry not, this is where we guide you through the various avenues you can trot down to further enrich your Akashic endeavors.

1. Books, But Not Just Any Books

You don't go picking up any random leaf while on a botanical exploration, do you? The same principle applies here. When you're looking to quench your Akashic thirst, select books that resonate not just with your mind, but your spirit. Forget the bestsellers; sometimes the most profound knowledge comes wrapped in unassuming covers.

2. Podcasts: The Invisible Mentors

Picture yourself in an ancient amphitheater, where sages and scholars impart wisdom. Now, transport that setting to the 21st century. Voila! You've got podcasts. Podcasts are like bottled wisdom, uncork them when you need a sip or gulp down an episode for a full dose of enlightenment. Seek out channels that delve into topics like quantum spirituality, metaphysics, and, of course, the Akashic Records.

3. Workshops: Your Spiritual Bootcamps

Ever tried mastering the art of bread-making or painting just by reading about it? There's a texture, a touch, a finesse to these things that only hands-on experience can offer. Similarly, Akashic Record workshops act as your spiritual bootcamps, offering practical techniques, guided journeys, and peer interactions. Sometimes it's more like a spiritual Comic-Con, minus the costumes—unless, of course, you wish to wear your cosmic robe!

4. Online Courses: The Magic School Bus for Adults

If the Hogwarts Express somehow missed you during childhood, don't fret. Online courses are the modern-day magic buses designed to whisk you away on a tour of the metaphysical landscapes. From introductory lessons to advanced modules, think of it as a choose-your-own-adventure kind of deal.

5. Sacred Texts: The Manuals of Yore

Think of sacred texts as the first-ever tablets—no, not iPads, but stone tablets. Scriptures, ancient manuscripts, or even age-old scrolls, these are the granddaddies of all spiritual teachings. If you're like an archaeologist sifting through layers of dirt to find a gem, these texts are worth the digging.

6. Ancestral Traditions: The Family Recipe for the Soul

You'd be surprised how many people overlook this treasure trove of wisdom. Family or ancestral practices often contain age-old wisdom, tailored specifically for you. Just like that secret family recipe that no restaurant can replicate, these teachings offer spiritual nourishment that's been custom-crafted across generations.

7. Guided Journals: Your Psychic Pen Pal

Imagine having a pen pal from another dimension. Guided journals serve a similar purpose, letting you maintain a dialogue with your spiritual self. It's a methodical way to jot down and revisit your Akashic experiences, analyze patterns, and decode messages.

8. The Network of Kindred Spirits: Connecting the Cosmic Dots

There's a good reason why shamans, priests, and wise women gathered in circles rather than in isolation. Spiritual networking isn't just about exchanging tips or favorite book titles; it's about reinforcing the tapestry of collective wisdom. Seek out forums, online communities, or local gatherings where you can meet like-minded souls.

What you've encountered so far in the Akashic Records is just the tip of the spiritual iceberg. As you plunge into these additional resources, picture yourself as a cosmic miner, equipped with both pickaxe and magnifying glass, chipping away at the surface but also looking closely at the nuances. Each book you read, each podcast you listen to, each workshop you attend layers another facet onto your multi-dimensional spiritual gemstone.

Oh, the thrill that comes with knowing there's a mountain of knowledge still left to climb! But remember, you're not just collecting artifacts for a spiritual showcase; you're adding tools to your ever-expanding cosmic toolbox. With every added resource, your connection with the Akashic Records becomes richer, deeper, and more textured—like adding new colors to your celestial palette.

So go ahead, pull out that cosmic library card and embark on a lifelong journey of metaphysical exploration.

You've got worlds to discover, and guess what? They've been waiting to discover you, too. Now, how exhilarating is that?

Suggested Books

"How to Read the Akashic Records: Accessing the Archive of the Soul and Its Journey" by Linda Howe

Linda Howe's book is considered one of the seminal works for those looking to delve into the Akashic Records. It offers practical instruction and provides a clear roadmap to accessing the records.

"The Akashic Records: Sacred Exploration of Your Soul's Journey Within the Wisdom of the Collective Consciousness" by Ernesto Ortiz

This book is praised for its depth and breadth, touching on history, methods, and how to use the Akashic Records for personal development. Ortiz provides a comprehensive view and specific practices.

"The Akashic Experience: Science and the Cosmic Memory Field" edited by Ervin Laszlo

This book offers a different take, exploring the Akashic Records through the lens of science and collective memory. It includes contributions from a variety of authors, each offering their own unique perspective on the topic.

"Akashic Records: Collective Keepers of Divine Expression" by Lumari

This book focuses on the Akashic Records as a source of divine wisdom and expression. It's a good pick for those interested in understanding the philosophical and spiritual dimensions of the Akashic Records.

"Discover Your Soul's Path Through the Akashic Records: Taking Your Life from Ordinary to Extraordinary" by Linda Howe

Another book by Linda Howe, this one goes beyond the basics and dives into how one can utilize the Akashic Records to discover one's life path. It aims to provide tools for transforming your life through the wisdom found in the records.

Final Blessings and Next Steps

Have you ever seen a caterpillar transform into a butterfly? There's no rush, no speeding up the process; it's all delicately orchestrated in nature's grand tapestry of life. In a similar vein, the spiritual journey you've embarked upon, especially in accessing the Akashic Records, should be savored in every little facet. You've come far, a path of challenges and revelations that are shaping you into the spiritual luminary you were destined to be. Now, as we approach the end of this book, let's unwind with final blessings and delve into the crucial next steps that await you.

Recapping Your Journey: Count Your Spiritual Blessings

Let's not underestimate the leaps you've made. Remember that this journey is more about the miles you've mentally and spiritually traversed than physically. Think back to your initial encounters with the Akashic realm; how have you changed since? Revisit your journal, if you kept one, and trace the spiritual breadcrumbs you've left for yourself.

The Ongoing Relationship with Your Guides

Your guides—be it Hermes, Thoth, or a spirit animal— aren't just mentors for a one-off project. No, they're like the wise elders of a tribe, continuously nudging you towards your highest self. It's like having a best friend who understands the unique layers of your soul. Continue the dialogue with them; they have much more to teach you.

The Empowered You: Channeling Akashic Wisdom

The more you practice, the less you'll need to rely on rigorous rituals to open the Akashic Records. Eventually, you'll be able to tap into these divine databases with more ease, like flipping through your favorite book to a well-worn chapter. It's like learning to ride a bike; you'll become more balanced with each practice.

Maintenance Work: Akashic Hygiene

Don't assume that just because you've accessed the Akashic Records, you're a sage ready to climb down the mountain. Spiritual work, akin to brushing your teeth or tuning an instrument, needs regular maintenance. Build a routine where you cleanse your spiritual palette through meditation or grounding exercises, so each Akashic visit is clear and uncluttered.

Explore Further: Akashic Tourism

You've dipped your toes into an ocean of cosmic consciousness; now it's time to explore different shores. Each record or guide provides different facets of wisdom. Why limit yourself? Think of it as trying out different courses at a celestial buffet.

Document and Share: Pen Down Your Wisdom

What good is wisdom if it remains cooped up? Consider sharing your experiences and insights with like-minded souls. This isn't boasting; it's contributing to the collective spiritual awareness. Don't you love it when a well-told story or advice comes your way just when you need it? Be that beacon for others.

The Final Invocation: Express Gratitude

Gratitude is the unsung hero of spiritual pursuits. As you wind down this chapter of your Akashic journey, express your heartfelt thanks to the guides, to the cosmic wisdom, and to yourself for taking courageous steps towards enlightenment. It's like thanking the host after a wonderful party; it leaves a warm feeling and an open invitation for a return.

Where To Now? Keep That Compass Handy

Your Akashic journey doesn't have to end when you close this book. Much like life, spiritual exploration is cyclical, not linear. What will you dive into next? Palmistry? Astral projection? As you flip through the pages of your next curiosity, rest assured that the Akashic Records will forever be your spiritual cornerstone, a divine library you can always return to.

So, why the caterpillar analogy? Because like that little creature, you are cocooned in your current stage of spiritual understanding. But the more you interact with the Akashic Records and apply these final blessings and next steps, the closer you are to breaking free and stretching your vibrant wings in the boundless skies of spiritual freedom.

What's stopping you? The universe is your playground, and you've just learned to climb the highest slide. Have fun, keep soaring, and may your next chapter be as enthralling as the words on these pages. With each slide down or climb up, may you gather more momentum, collecting orbs of wisdom along the way. Go ahead, the next slide awaits. And trust me, you'll want to experience the thrill again and again.

In conclusion, the gratitude we hold for the guidance and wisdom of Greek God Hermes is immeasurable. As we embark on our journey to unveil the mysteries of the Akashic Records, Hermes serves as our loyal guide, leading us to profound self-discovery, healing, and transformation. With his divine connection and unparalleled knowledge, we are empowered to embrace our true selves and live a life aligned with our soul's purpose.

Here's to your endless cosmic journey, my friend.

CHAPTER TWELVE

Glossary of Terms

Akashic Records

The celestial databases storing all universal experiences, events, and emotions, like an infinite, spiritual library.

Akashic Tourism

The exploration of different records or guides within the Akashic realm, akin to sampling different courses at a celestial buffet.

Akashic Hygiene

The practice of regular spiritual cleansing to maintain clear and uncluttered access to the Akashic Records.

Astral Projection

The experience of separating the astral body from the physical body to journey in the astral plane.

Celestial Buffet

A metaphorical way to describe the diverse opportunities for learning and experiences within the spiritual realm.

Channeling

The act of connecting with a spiritual entity or energy, serving as a conduit for the transfer of information or healing.

Cosmic Consciousness

The higher plane of consciousness that connects all beings, accessible through spiritual practice.

Cosmic Journey

Your personal path of spiritual growth and exploration, often used interchangeably with 'spiritual journey'.

Divine Databases

Another term for the Akashic Records, emphasizing their function as a vast repository of universal knowledge.

Enlightenment

The ultimate goal of many spiritual practices; a state of understanding and peace, free from the cycle of rebirth and suffering.

Grounding Exercises

Methods used to balance energy and connect with the Earth, often employed before and after spiritual work like accessing the Akashic Records.

Invocation

A ritualistic call to a higher power, guide, or spirit for assistance or blessing.

Meditation

A practice to quiet the mind and achieve higher states of consciousness, often used as a gateway to accessing the Akashic Records.

Palmistry

The practice of interpreting the lines on a person's palm to learn about their character and future prospects.

Ritual

A structured series of actions or spells conducted to achieve a specific spiritual outcome.

Sage

A person endowed with profound wisdom and spiritual insight, often considered a teacher or mentor.

Spiritual Breadcrumbs

Personal markers or significant experiences that guide you on your spiritual journey.

Spiritual Cornerstone

A foundational practice or belief that shapes and supports your spiritual journey; the Akashic Records serve this function for many.

Spiritual Luminary

Someone who lights the way in spiritual understanding, often guiding others on their journeys.

Spiritual Palette

Your unique collection of spiritual experiences, gifts, and challenges.

Spirit Animal

An animal that appears as a form of guide, bringing messages or offering assistance on your spiritual journey.

Spirit Guide

Non-physical entities that offer guidance, protection, and teachings during your spiritual journey. I my case, they can be rather sarcastic.

Tribe

Your spiritual community or circle, often consisting of like-minded individuals who support you in your cosmic journey.

Wise Elders

Mature, experienced spiritual guides who offer wisdom and advice, sometimes appearing in the form of ancestors or other respected figures in your journey.

ABOUT THE AUTHOR

About The Author

Dave is an author of adult fantasy (The Furies series) as well as author of occult books about magick.

David began working ritual magick back in the 1970s. He took a brief break, then used the power of this magick to create a photography career which took him to Los Angeles and work as a photographer for multiple magazines.

David has studied magick in all forms, and in 2018, released a three-part magick instruction course in High Magick. Thousands of students have benefited from David's unique teaching style, making ceremonial magick accessible to everyone.

This book on Hermes is number 8 in his Grecian Magik Series. Dave also has a series on High Magick, exploring the aspects of ceremonial magick with deities and daemons of all pantheons.

Dave's Facebook Page:
https://www.facebook.com/DavePsychic/

Secrets of Magick Facebook Group:
https://www.facebook.com/groups/secretsofmagick

Join the Grecian Magick Facebook group!
https://www.facebook.com/groups/grecianmagick

Dave's webpage, book readings and his services:
https://davepsychic.com
Then his e-learning website for magik classes
https://highmagikacademy.com

Magick Books by David Thompson

Available as EPUB, Paperback and Hardcover (*)

High Magick Series
- High Magick 101
- Daemons of High Magick

- Daemons and the Law of Attraction*
- Magick of Astaroth*
- Daemons of Fortune*
- Lilith: Goddess of Darkness and Light*
- Asmodeus King of Daemons*
- Daemons of Fortune*
- Divinator's Handbook
- Goddesses of High Magik

Grecian Magick Series

- Magick of Apollo
- Magick of Hermes
- Magick of Aphrodite
- Magick of Fortuna*
- Greco-Roman Wealth Magick*
- Magick of the Sirens/Magick of the Muses

Fiction Novels by David Thompson

The Furies Series

- Angels of Vengeance
- Descent into Tartarus
- Furies: Beginnings
- Brianna: Making of a Fury